ALASKA WILD FLOWERS

Field of *Lupinus nootkatensis*, near Juneau,
with Mendenhall Glacier in the background

ALASKA WILD FLOWERS

By

ADA WHITE SHARPLES

STANFORD UNIVERSITY PRESS
STANFORD UNIVERSITY, CALIFORNIA

STANFORD UNIVERSITY PRESS
STANFORD, CALIFORNIA
LONDON: OXFORD UNIVERSITY PRESS

Second printing, July 1958
PRINTED IN THE UNITED STATES OF AMERICA

Library of Congress Catalog Card Number: 38-27490

PREFACE

To be able to call the plants by name makes them a hundredfold more sweet and intimate. Naming things is one of the oldest and simplest of human pastimes.

—HENRY VAN DYKE, in *Little Rivers*

Many years ago when I first came to Alaska, Nature's garden of wild flowers, so lavishly strewn over mountains and valleys, interested me exceedingly. Yet very little written material on the subject was available, and I lacked the technical knowledge required to make my own identifications. "What is its name?" was my continual plaintive cry.

Then at Juneau I met Mr. J. P. Anderson, a graduate of Iowa State College and one of the first resident scientists to undertake an exhaustive collection and classification of the flora of Alaska. His large herbarium, which has grown prodigiously since then, was generously offered me for studying, and I began. Thanks largely to his kindness and to his patience in answering my questions, this book has now been prepared.

Since Alaska covers approximately the same number of degrees of latitude and longitude as the entire United States, its flora is of great variety. What is roughly termed the Interior, as distinguished from the Coast region, extends from the Arctic Circle south approximately to Talkeetna, east to Eagle, and west to the far boundary of Mount McKinley Park. There the winters are long, with a plentiful snowfall, and for months the thermometer stays below the zero mark. Summer arrives precipitately, spring and autumn being almost negligible; and for a month or two there is no night there. In these long sunlit days the vegetation grows apace. The heavy, brooding evergreen forests of the Coast region have given place to the lighter growth of birch and poplar, with willows and alders along the water courses. There tower mountain ranges whose peaks are among the highest in the world, furnishing a home for many

v

choice alpines, such as the Androsaces, Eritrichiums, Anemones, and Saxifrages. Where the fertile forested valleys are spread, Aconites and Delphiniums reach great height, and wild berries and wild roses flourish.

From Point Barrow, the northernmost settlement on the North American continent, southward along the deep indentations and far-flung peninsulas, including the Nome district, and down the coast, embracing the outer segment of the Aleutian Islands, the mountains have receded many miles from the shore. This leaves a wide, flat tundra, where the Arctic Poppy (*Papaver radicatum*), the Forget-me-not (*Myosotis alpestris*), the *Iris setosa*, Lupinus spp., the *Kalmia microphylla*, the Ledums, the *Fritillaria camschatcensis*, and various others bloom in riotous profusion, reveling in the long hours of daylight and the plentiful moisture at their feet.

Where the Yukon, the Kuskokwim, the Nushagak, and other rivers flow sluggishly through the treeless plain to the ocean, the tundra country extends far back, and much of the swamp is given over to rankly growing grasses.

From the Alaska Peninsula southward the mountains draw nigh to the sea again and the copious rainfall begins, exerting its influence on the vegetation. The mountainsides are clothed with a dense growth of hemlock and spruce, with an undergrowth like a tropical jungle, including many berry-bearing shrubs such as Devil's Club and Elder, and various species of Ribes, Rubus, and Vaccinium. Above the timber line on exposed slopes are spread matted rugs of dwarf flowering shrubs, including the Cassiopes, *Empetrum nigrum*, Phyllodoce, *Diapensia lapponica*, and *Arctostaphylos Uva-ursi*; and in alpine meadows grow the herbaceous Gentians, Campanulas, Dryas, and a host of others. Some of these continue along the coast to Ketchikan, and others are succeeded by plants which require more equable conditions.

In attempting here to give the range of the different species, I do not maintain that the sections noted are the only localities in which each may be found. Neither do I claim that this volume completely covers the flora of Alaska. Only the southern section of the Territory, which is the more acces-

vi

sible, has been thoroughly botanized. In the Interior and northern sections, vast areas of which no white man has ever trod, a wealth of plant life is waiting to be collected and classified. Thus Alaska is truly a botanists' paradise.

Many government school teachers and nurses in out-of-the-way places have aided me in collecting specimens. Others to whom I am deeply indebted are: Dr. Eric Hulten of the University of Lund, Sweden, who spent the season of 1931 in botanical research in Alaska; Mrs. Jessie Cook Anderson, of Caribou Island, Skilak Lake; Mrs. Nellie Erskine, of Kodiak; Mrs. Mamie Elwell, of Seward; Mrs. Elsie Coats, of Chitina; Superintendent Harry Liek, of Mount McKinley Park, and Mrs. Liek; and scores of others who have generously given assistance and encouragement.

The photographs are the work of the better part of three summers spent in tramping mountain trails and wading through mosquito-infested swamps with my friend and fellow-enthusiast, Maxcine Williams, as companion.

The arrangement of both photographs and text is alphabetical by species; and it has seemed unnecessary to provide a key. The index is devised to aid the amateur.

I realize the weakness of attempting to express scientific truth in simpler language than that of the truth itself, but in offering this book my desire has been to fill the need of the army of wild-flower lovers, including the school child and the casual visitor to Alaska, who find themselves floundering helplessly among the technical terms of the usual botanical descriptions in search of the answer to their query: "What is its name?"

A. W. S.

Juneau, Alaska
March 1, 1938

vii

ALASKA WILD FLOWERS

To the true lover of Nature wild flowers have a charm which no garden can equal. Cultivated plants are but a living herbarium. They surpass, no doubt, the dried specimens of a museum, but, lovely as they are, they can be no more compared with the natural vegetation of our woods and fields than the captives in the zoölogical gardens with the same wild species in their native forests and mountains.

—SIR JOHN LUBBOCK, in *Beauties of Nature*

ACER (classical Latin name). Aceraceae. "Maple." Well-known trees and shrubs, with characteristic, easily distinguished foliage.

A. Douglasii. "Dwarf Maple," a small tree occurring sparingly in Southeastern Alaska. Closely allied to the "Vine Maple" of Washington and Oregon.

A. macrophyllum. "Big-Leaf Maple." A beautiful shade tree, entering southern Alaska.

ACHILLEA (its virtues said to have been discovered by Achilles). Compositae. "Millfoil," "Yarrow." Herbaceous perennials; foliage has a strong, characteristic odor.

A. borealis. A weedy plant of the roadsides and vacant town lots. Very common in all sections of Alaska. Erect branching plant, from 8 inches to 2 feet. Leaves very finely dissected. Flowers white, sometimes tinged with rose, in terminal corymbs. (Illus. p. 2.)

A. lanulosa. Smaller than above. Woolly leaves and stem. Interior.

A. multiflora. Tall, slender. Leaves less divided than the two above. Interior.

1

Achillea borealis
Aconitum Chamissonianum

Actaea arguta
Adiantum pedatum, var. *aleuticum*

3

ACONITUM. Ranunculaceae. A group characterized by its showy flowers and attractive palmate foliage. The common name, "Monkshood," is bestowed because of the distinguishing feature of the whole genus in the one enlarged sepal noticeably like a helmet or hood. In the hood the nectaries are neatly tucked away and protected from dampness. Long tongues are necessary to reach the honey and it is largely dependent upon bumblebees and hummingbirds for pollinization.

A. Chamissonianum. This very dark-blue species grows among the grasses and herbs of moist alpine meadows. Altitude is a factor in determining its height, and above the timber line at about 3,000 feet it is much shorter than the 3-foot spikes found at sea level. Southeastern Alaska. (Illus. p. 2.)

A. delphinifolium. Somewhat taller than the one above and of sturdier growth. As indicated by the specific name, the foliage is quite similar to that of its near relative, the Delphinium. Flowers deep purplish blue. Common in the Nome section and the Interior as far south as Cordova.

A. kamtschaticum and *A. maximum* are found on the Aleutian Islands.

ACONOGONUM (intermediate between the Knotweeds [Polygonum] and the Docks [Rumex]). The flower clusters of Aconogonum somewhat resemble those of the garden Rhubarb. There is no recognized common name for this plant.

A. phytalaccaefolium. Grows 2 to 4 feet tall. Interior.

ACTAEA (ancient name of Elder, transferred by Linnaeus). Ranunculaceae. "Baneberry."

A. arguta. Height 1½ to 2 feet; compound leaves with five leaflets, deeply incised. Flowers small, creamy white, in terminal racemes; numerous prominent stamens. Followed by grape-like bunches of showy, bright-red berries. Attains a sturdy growth in rich damp woods. Southeastern Alaska. (Illus. p. 3.)

4

A. eburnea. Similar to the preceding except that its berries are pure white, appearing exactly as if made of porcelain. Same range as above, sometimes growing with it.

ADIANTUM (Greek, "unwetted"). Polypodiaceae. "Maidenhair Fern."

A. pedatum, var. ***aleuticum.*** A variety of the common "Maidenhair," sometimes called the "Five-Finger Fern," found in many parts of the United States. One of the most beautiful of all ferns. The erect fronds are from 12 to 40 inches long, with polished, purplish-brown leafstalks. Segments close, oblong, and deeply cleft. The polished stipes or stems are much prized by the natives of Alaska for decorating baskets. Common in Southeastern Alaska. (Illus. p. 3.)

ALLIUM (ancient Latin name of garlic). Liliaceae. Bulbous plants, comprising also the Onion and Chives of the vegetable gardens.

A. sibericum. Large form of the common garden chives. Leaves numerous, slender. Scapes equaling the leaves. Flowers bright lavender pink, small and many, in a globular head. Found abundantly in Nome and Interior regions.

ALNUS (the ancient Latin name). Betulaceae. "Alder." Deciduous trees or shrubs. Flowers are catkins, appearing before the leaves. The three species named are found in almost every part of the Territory.

A. fruticosa. A thicket-forming shrub.

A. oregona (A. rubra). Large hardwood tree, valuable as timber. "Red Alder." Widely distributed.

A. sinuata. Attains considerable height, but is really a shrubby form. Inclined to branch thickly from the base. Grows in dense thickets above the timber line, where it is much dwarfed. Similar in manner of growth to *A. fruticosa,* but has narrower leaves. (Illus. p. 6.)

5

Alnus sinuata
Anaphalis angustifolium

Andromeda polifolia
Anemone globosa

ALSINE (Greek from "grove," where some species grow). Caryophyllaceae. There is much disagreement among botanists as to the standing of this genus. Some refer to it as Arenaria, and others use it to replace Stellaria. The "Chickweeds"; slender, smooth little plants, with many starlike, white flowers.

A. laeta and *A. stellaria.* Inconspicuous, small-flowered weedy species, found in various parts of the Territory. Both are found in Mount McKinley Park.

AMELANCHIER (said to be a Savoy name). Rosaceae. Deciduous, berry-bearing shrubs.

A. florida. "Serviceberry" or "Juneberry." Sometimes attains 10 feet. Stout, upright branches; oval leaves, sharply toothed. Racemes of white flowers, followed by black fruit. Fruit is of very good quality and similar to cultivated forms. Interior.

ANAPHALIS (Greek name of a similar plant). Compositae.

A. angustifolium. "Pearly Everlasting." A white, woolly, perennial herb, with heads of yellow disk flowers but no ray flowers, surrounded by pure-white, papery bracts, in corymbs. Stems usually about a foot high; leaves lance-shaped, green above. The stems and under side of the leaves are white, with soft, loose, cottony hairs. Grows along roadsides and in open fields, Southeastern Alaska. (Illus. p. 6.)

A. subalpina. Quite similar to the preceding except that its leaves are downy on both sides. Kodiak. Glacier Bay.

ANDROMEDA (Greek mythological name). Ericaceae. "Bog Rosemary." Low evergreen shrubs of the muskeg swamps.

A. polifolia. Attains height of about one foot. Leaves very narrow, whitish beneath. Beautiful nodding blossoms on long pedicels, of an enchanting shade of pink. The blossoms have been described as "little classic alabaster urns." (Illus. p. 7.)

ANDROSACE (old Greek name of no significance here). Primulaceae. "Rock Jasmine." Small, tufted plants, usually found at high altitudes, where there is abundant moisture which drains quickly away. Have the shining, intense quality of all true alpines.

A. Chamaejasme (A. Lehmanniana). A diminutive caespitose plant, with rosettes of small hairy leaves, from each of which a stem about an inch long is sent up. This bears a headlike umbel of fragrant, cream-colored flowers. The eye of each flower is at first yellow, but turns pink with age. Abundant on rocky alpine slopes of the Interior.

A. septrionalis. Small alpine plant with naked flower stems sometimes 6 inches long, from rosettes of basal leaves. Inflorescence an umbel with numerous, tiny, starlike, white blossoms. Found in the vicinity of Fairbanks.

ANEMONE (from the Greek word meaning "wind"; hence the common name, "Windflower"). Ranunculaceae. Distinguished from the Buttercups by having no corolla but only a calyx with sepals colored like petals.

A. globosa. A slender plant with very finely divided foliage. Solitary white, pink, or blue flowers. Stems, leaves, and sepals hairy. Abundant in the subalpine zones in the Interior; rare in southern portion of the Territory. (Illus. p. 7.)

A. narcissiflora. The specific name is bestowed because of the resemblance of the individual flower to a poet's narcissus in the thick-textured white sepals and cluster of yellow stamens. The flowers grow several in an umbel, on stems from 8 to 10 inches long. This beautiful flower is found above the timber line at an altitude of around 2,500 feet, and grows thickly over wide areas. In June a mountain slope on which it grows appears covered with snow and is a sight not easily forgotten. In practically every part of the Territory. (Illus. p. 10.)

10

Anemone narcissiflora
Anemone parviflora

Antennaria pallida
Antennaria rosea

11

A. parviflora. Dwarf species of high altitudes. Tufted growth. Flowers white, shaded purple on outside, large in proportion to size of plant. Occurs in every part of the Territory. (Illus. p. 10.)

A. Richardsonii. Small plant. Brilliant yellow blossoms. Often taken for a Buttercup. Over entire Coast region and the Interior.

ANGELICA (supposed to have angelic healing qualities). Umbelliferae. Stout plants, growing in meadows and fields. Sometimes confused with Heracleum, with which it often grows, but its blooming time is later. It is also distinguished by the leaves, which are three-branched, then twice-pinnate, with finely toothed leaflets. Stems and underneath leaves smooth. White flowers in large umbels.

A. genuflexa. As indicated by the name, the joint of the leaf is like a bent knee. All parts of the Territory.

ANTENNARIA (pappus likened to antennae). Compositae. Small, woolly, perennial plants. Not showy, but of attractive, neat growth. Leaves tufted and flat growing. Erect stems, bearing heads of inconspicuous flowers. "Cat's Ear," "Ladies' Tobacco," "Pussy Toes."

A. borealis and *A. monocephala* are dwarfs of much the same aspect as *A. pallida.* Tufted alpines. Interior.

A. pallida. Common in Southeastern Alaska, its woolly white tufts spreading in a thick carpet over rocky exposed places. Flowers white, on leafy stems, and 3 inches tall. On mountain summits of the Interior and Southeastern Alaska. (Illus. p. 11.)

A. pulcherrima. One to two feet tall. The one Alaska species that is not tufted. Long lanceolate leaves. Whole plant densely downy. A woodland species of the Interior.

A. rosea. Taller than *A. pallida,* and less common. Flowers are an attractive pink. Interior and Southeastern Alaska. (Illus. p. 11.)

AQUILEGIA (from *aquilegus,* "water-drawer"; not *aquila,* "eagle"). Ranunculaceae. Common name "Columbine." Easily recognized by its showy, five-petaled flowers. Petals concave, and produced backward between the sepals, forming a hollow spur. Sepals colored like petals. Numerous stamens. Attractive glaucous foliage. Root and stem leaves compound.

A. formosa. One of the most beautiful and abundant of Alaska wild flowers. Found in almost all parts of the Territory and especially in the Southeastern section. Height, 2 to 3 feet. Flowers lacquer-red and yellow, gracefully swaying on slender stalks above the large basal clump of leaves. (Illus. p. 14.)

ARABIS (Arabia). Cruciferae. "Rock Cress." Small perennials, thriving in poor soil. Inconspicuous white flowers, mostly in terminal spikes.

A. ambigua and *A. hyrata,* var. *kamtschatica* are near synonymous. Somewhat weedy little plants occurring in every part of the Territory. *A. hirsuta* is also this type of plant.

A. retrofracta is a large weed of the Interior.

ARCTERANTHIS Cooleyae. Ranunculaceae. Placed by some botanists in the Ranunculus genus, as it is very similar in some respects to the common Buttercup. The specific name is in honor of Miss Grace E. Cooley, a botanist who first collected the plant near Juneau.

Thick-textured, many-petaled blossoms of lacquered yellow, very fragrant, spring from a tuft of vigorous, much-divided foliage. The flowers follow close on the heels of the vanishing snow at high altitudes. Flowers and leaves are produced simultaneously. Often the yellow tint of the flowers may be seen through the watery snow at the edge of a diminishing snow field. Found only in Southeastern Alaska. (Illus. p. 14.)

14

Aquilegia formosa
Arcteranthis Cooleyae

Arnica latifolia
Asplenium Trichomanes

ARCTOSTAPHYLOS (from Greek "bear" and grape"). Ericaceae. Dwarf, broad-leaved evergreen.

A. Uva-ursi. "Kinnikinnick." Trailing evergreen shrub, which often completely covers the ground over a considerable area. The leaves are hard and firm, distinctly petioled, and about half an inch or more long. Flowers pink. Its red berries are sometimes called "Chipmunk's apples" by children. The shreddy, reddish bark of the stems suggests its relationship to the Manzanita of the Pacific Coast. Interior. Rarely in Southeastern Alaska.

ARCTOUS (Greek "boreal," referring to its distribution). Small subshrubs of high altitudes.

A. alpinus. "Black Bearberry." Prostrate shrub with shreddy bark. Thin, deciduous leaves clustered toward the end of the branches. Small, white flowers, followed by bluish-black berries. Much the aspect of trailing willows of high altitudes.

A. erythrocarpa. Quite similar to the preceding but with red berries. "Red Bearberry."
Both are found in the Interior and in Southeastern Alaska.

ARENARIA. "Sandwort." Caryophyllaceae. Small, tufted perennials, with white flowers.

A. arctica (Minuarta arctica). Heavy tuft, with single taproot; flowers large. Alpine regions of the Interior and the Aleutian Islands.

A. macrocarpa. Very similar to the preceding. Interior.

A. propinqua. Tiny plant of slender growth. At home in low wet ground in Southeastern Alaska and Interior.

A. stricta. Dense tuft of grassy foliage spread out from a single taproot. Flowers numerous and small. Interior.

16

ARNICA (ancient name). Compositae. Perennial herbs with clustered root leaves and large long-peduncled yellow heads of daisylike flowers, growing usually at high altitudes. Flower centers as well as ray flowers are in various shades of yellow. Stem leaves usually in pairs. The lotion called "Arnica" and used extensively in medicine is an extract from the European species, *A. montana.*

A. alpina. Basal leaves lanceolate. Entire plant hairy. From 1–3 flower heads of pale yellow on stems which attain two feet. Interior.

A. borealis. The type was first collected by J. P. Anderson near Juneau in 1917. Heads 3–7 with light orange rays on stems 12–18 inches. Lanceolate leaves.

A. brevifolia. A small alpine species found in many parts of the Interior. Heads solitary, slightly nodding, bright yellow, on 5-inch stems. Densely hairy.

A. chamissonis. A tall species with stem leaves in pairs, sparingly hairy. Leaves lanceolate. Flowers in heads of 5–20, bright yellow. Southwestern Alaska and Interior.

A. kodiakensis. Stem about 10 inches. Stem leaves about 4 pairs, sparingly pubescent. Flowers in heads of 3–5. Rays orange yellow. Center yellowish-brown. Kodiak Island and parts of the Interior.

A. latifolia. Basal leaves oval, long-petioled. Stem leaves 3–5 pairs, the lower short-petioled, the upper sessile. Bright yellow heads, 1–5 in corymb. Southeastern Alaska. (Illus. p. 15.)

A. lessingii. Stem 3–5 inches, densely clothed with brown hairs. Basal leaves small, spatulate; stem leaves 2–4 pairs near base, smooth above, hairy beneath. Yellow heads solitary, nodding. Rays deeply toothed. Southwestern Alaska and Interior.

A. obtusifolia. Stem 3–6 inches; basal leaves small, spatulate; stem leaves usually 3 pairs. Slightly hairy. Heads solitary, nodding, bright yellow. Aleutian Islands.

17

Aster foliaceus
Aster siberica

Boschniakia glabra
Caltha asarifolia

19

A. unalaschensis. Stem 3–6 inches, with about 3 pairs of leaves. Basal and stem leaves oblong. Plant somewhat hairy. Head solitary. Rays bright yellow; center light brown. Reported at Unalaska and on islands in Bering Sea.

Other species found in Alaska include *A. cordifolia, A. elongata, A. leptocaulis, A. mendenhallii, A. mollis, A. nutans, A. oligolepis,* and *A. rivularis.*

ARTEMISIA (Artemisia, wife of Mausolus). Compositae. "Wormwood," "Dusty Miller." Some species in western United States are known as "Sagebrush."

A. arctica. Height is ruled by exposure; sometimes attains 18 inches. Leaves alternate, much dissected. Very little down. Flowers in terminal spike, small, greenish, and inconspicuous. Found above timber line generally, in thin gravelly soil. Interior and Southwestern and Southeastern Alaska.

A. frigida. Leaves, stems, and flowers gray. Basal leaves few. Stems covered with short leaves, very finely dissected. Panicle of flowers about half of stem. Dry hillsides of Interior.

A. spithamaea. Open grasslands of the Interior. Dwarf, tufted. Downy white. Flowers in spike. Leaves finely dissected.

A. tilesii, var. ***unalaschensis.*** A bold plant found at sea level, where it attains several feet in height in rich, moist humus. Large, oak-shaped leaves, dark olive-green above, downy white beneath. Flowers in long stiff panicle. Particularly abundant on Aleutian Islands and Coast northward.

ASPLENIUM (Greek—"not the spleen"—referring to supposed medicinal properties). Polypodiaceae.

A. Trichomanes. Similar to *A. viride* except leafstalk shining black. (Illus. p. 15.)

A. viride. A very small fern growing among the rocks. Neat symmetrical growth. Distinguished by green leafstalk.

Both found in Southeastern Alaska.

20

ASTER (a star). Compositae. Marked by a center cluster of tubular flowers surrounded by numerous long narrow rays, leafy stems, and leaves always alternate.

A. foliaceus. A friendly plant, seeking the roadsides and byways of man. Its center is yellow, with long narrow purple rays, somewhat ragged in appearance. It is a vigorous plant, thickly branched and leafy. Although not showy, the soft autumnal hazy purple of a large mass of this, with Goldenrod as companion, is very effective. The appearance of these two wayside flowers is the first indication that the northern summer is nearing the end. Southeastern Alaska, Aleutian Islands. (Illus. p. 18.)

A. junceus. Flowers purple or white in terminal panicles in stems from 6 to 18 inches. Slender, branching. Wet roadsides. Circle Hot Springs. Matanuska.

A. siberica. Profuse in Southwestern Alaska and Interior, also at Nome. Usually about one foot tall. Each stem terminating in one to several flowers. Rays pinkish violet; yellow disk. (Illus. p. 18.)

ASTRAGALUS (Greek name). Leguminosae. "Milk Vetch," "Cow Weed." Separated from the "Locoweed" (*Oxytropis*) by the shape of the keel, which in this group is blunt at the end. All species have vetch-like, pinnate, compound foliage and lax flower stems springing from the crown. Pea-shaped flowers in terminal racemes.

A. alpinus. Purple-tinted flowers; small plant. Found in almost every section of Alaska. Level meadows.

A. americanus. Vigorous; large leaves; white-flowered. In the vicinity of McCarthy and other parts of the Interior.

A. falcata. Distinctive. Leaves very small. Tufted growth. Flowers and fruit large. Gravelly plains of the Interior.

A. umbellatus. A dwarf alpine of the Interior, with yellowish flowers.

Calypso bulbosa
Campanula lasiocarpa, var. *alpina*

Campanula petiolata
Cassiope lycopodioides

ATHYRIUM. Polypodiaceae. A genus of coarse, tall ferns.

A. cyclosorum. "Brake." Fronds in a crown, slightly narrowed toward base. Yellowish-green; strong growing; often 3 to 5 feet.

BARBAREA (from the old name, "Herb of St. Barbara"). Cruciferae. Hardy biennials with yellow flowers, allied to water cress and horse-radish.

B. stricta. Large, smooth leaves. Small, yellow flowers in loose head. All parts of the Territory.

BETULA (ancient Latin name). Betulaceae. "Birch." Ornamental deciduous trees or shrubs, characterized by their slender, graceful habit and delicate foliage.

B. glandulifera. Dwarf. An ornamental shrub from 1 to 4 feet. Leaves short-petioled and round, toothed, brilliantly colored in autumn. Occurs in northern Coast regions and the Interior.

B. kenaica. The brown-barked or Kenai birch, together with *B. alaskana,* the Alaska white-barked birch, comprises most of the deciduous forests of the Interior.

BLITUM capitatum. Chenopodiaceae. "Strawberry Blite." A fleshy, branched annual herb that is found in moist mountain valleys. It grows 8 to 20 inches high and is smooth throughout. The leaves are spear-shaped and sharply toothed. The enlarged fleshy floral envelopes form large globular clusters in the axils of the leaves, and turn bright red, somewhat resembling strawberries. Interior.

BOSCHNIAKIA (after Boschniak, a Russian botanist). Orobanchaceae.

B. glabra. A parasite on the roots of Alder. Woody, cone-like spike, 6 to 8 inches tall, covered with clustered red or brown scales, with numerous inconspicuous flowers. Eaten by the Indians, who call it "Poque." Southeastern Alaska and parts of the Interior. (Illus. p. 19.)

24

BOTRYCHIUM (from Greek, *botrys*, a bunch of grapes, from the appearance of the clustered sporangi). "Grape Fern," "Moonwort." A genus of small ferns. Rootstock short, erect, with clustered fleshy roots; the bud for next year's frond embedded in the base of the stalk. The frond with sterile and fertile segments; sterile segments 1–3 pinnate, the fertile bearing naked sporangi in two rows.

B. lanceolatum. Occurs on high mountains near Juneau and other parts of Southeastern Alaska.

B. Lunaria. In open grassland of the Interior.

B. neglectum. Among grass near beach and in alpine meadows of the Interior.

BUPLEURUM (Greek "ox" and "rib"; of no obvious application). Umbelliferae. "Thorough Wax."

B. americanum. Dwarf, somewhat weedy plants, with umbels of small yellow flowers. Common in dry sterile places, Alaska Peninsula and northward.

CALLA (ancient name of obscure meaning). Araceae. A monotypic genus.

C. palustris. "Water Arum." Herb with creeping rhizome, growing in shallow water. Blossom has form and appearance of small florist's calla lily, which, however, is of another genus. Interior.

CALTHA (Latin name of the Marigold). Ranunculaceae. "Marsh Marigold." Succulent, perennial marsh plants, which flourish near running water.

C. asarifolia. Spreads rapidly from stolons; strong fibrous roots. Large, rounded-cordate leaves. Flowers deep yellow, 1–2 inches across, in racemes. No petals; sepals petallike; many stamens. Free blooming and very beautiful. Southwestern and Southeastern Alaska. (Illus. p. 19.)

Cassiope Mertensiana
Castilleja pallida

Castelleja parviflora
Cerastium alpinum

C. biflora. White-flowered, not stoloniferous. Grows in low marshes and at margins of ponds, plentifully around Ketchikan and as far north as Sitka.

C. leptosepala. "Alpine Marsh Marigold"; white-flowered. Found at high altitudes in marshes formed by melting snow. Juneau and northward.

CALYPSO (from the Greek goddess, whose name signifies "concealment," referring to its rarity and beauty). Orchidaceae. "Fairy Slipper." A monotypic genus.

C. bulbosa. The "Fairy Slipper" is borne on a four-inch stem above a single pleated leaf. The drooping lip is larger than the rest of the flower and forms the toe of the slipper or sac. The lidlike heel is formed of the anther. Five ascending petals and sepals, which are similar, ornament the top of the flower. The sac is soft and downy, faintly mottled with brown and purple, and its throat is lined with yellow velvet. The whole forms a dainty rose-hued slipper obviously fashioned for a fairy's foot. They appear profusely on certain small islands in Southeastern Alaska, growing in little groups in moss in shady woods. Sisters Island, Brothers Island, and Turnabout Island are literally covered with these exotic little plants. (Illus. p. 22.)

CAMPANULA (Latin, "little bell," from the shape of the corolla in some species). Campanulaceae. "Blue Bell." Five sepals, five stamens, and five-lobed corolla. Perhaps the best-loved of all Alaska wild flowers. Seeds are emitted by 3 to 5 valves at the base of the capsule.

C. alaskana. Stem leaves numerous and somewhat hairy. Slender growing. Found in profusion in many localities in Southeastern Alaska growing from rock crevices along the seashore. Also grows above the timber line, but does not appear to have an intermediate range. Violet-blue bells.

C. heterodoxa. A lowland species. Sometimes confused with *C. petiolata,* but the plant is sturdier, taller, and has stiffer upright stems. Also the stems are leafy. Profuse in most sections of the Territory.

28

C. lasiocarpa, var. *alpina.* Root leaves form a tiny basal slump, above which the relatively large bells appear on lax stems not more than 3 inches tall. Stem and calyx are covered with thick hairs. The wide-open bells are a bright, clear indigo blue, with a dark line down the center of each petal. Found only at high altitudes, growing in the most meager gravelly soil. Has a wide range over most of the Territory. (Illus. p. 22.)

C. petiolata. Very similar to the well-known *C. rotundiflora,* native of Europe as well as of North America. In July the small plant hangs out a carillon of beautiful violet-blue bells on lax, wiry stems from crevices of shale cliffs in which it delights to grow. In all her experience in photographing wild flowers the writer found this the most difficult subject. Even when there is no perceptible breeze, the little tinkling bells keep up a continual dancing movement. The small, tufted root leaves are kidney-shaped, petiolate, and leathery. Stem leaves are few, slender, and lanceolate. This species is found in the vicinity of Juneau and in other sections of the Territory. (Illus. p. 23.)

C. uniflora. A distinct species, in that the corolla is not bell-shaped. Petals ½-inch long emerge from the calyx in a tight cluster. A single flower nods on each stem above a basal clump of long, lance-shaped, leathery leaves. Grows among Dryas and *Silene acaulis* in many sections of the Interior.

CARDAMINE (Greek name for a cress). Cruciferae. "Bitter Cress."

C. bellidifolia. Neat, tufted alpine, growing among rocks at high altitude. From 1 to 3 inches tall. Numerous, small, white flowers. Southeastern Alaska and the Interior.

C. pratensis. "Cuckoo Flower." Grows 6–10 inches. Foliage scant. Terminal cluster of pinkish lavender flowers, each about ¾ inch across. Swampy soil, all along the coast.

Chrysanthemum arcticum
Cicuta Douglasii

Cladothamnus pyrolaeflorus
Claytonia siberica

31

CASSIOPE (Greek mythological name). Ericaceae. Dwarf, prostrate, evergreen shrubs with slender creeping stems which suggest "Club Moss" in their habit. At home on top of the very highest peaks. The charm of this intrepid little member of the heath family greatly impressed John Muir, and his writings contain many references to what is said to have been his favorite flower. Characterized by solitary, waxy flowers, very similar to those of the Lily-of-the-Valley, nodding on short peduncles which spring from the axils of the leaves.

C. lycopodioides. Small, compact-growing, with very slender branches. Leaves about ⅛ inch long, overlapping and clasping the stem in the manner of scales. The tiny, cuplike blossoms are milk-white. The rarest and smallest of this group. Found sparingly at high altitudes in Southeastern and Southwestern Alaska. (Illus. p. 23.)

C. Mertensiana. Flowers cream-white, shaded with pink, the rim of the tiny cup recurved. Manner of growth quite similar to the preceding, but much more vigorous. Often found growing in a tangle along with *Vaccinium uliginosum* and *Empetrum nigrum.* Common on high mountains from Skagway southward. (Illus. p. 26.)

C. tetragona. This is the Cassiope of the Interior, where it is very abundant. Quite similar to *C. Mertensiana.*

CASTILLEJA (obtains its name from a Spanish botanist, D. Castillejo). Scrophulariaceae. "Indian Paintbrush." Herbs with inconspicuous flowers and showy bracts in terminal heads or spikes. More or less root-parasitic, and for this reason difficult to transplant unless introduced along with some of the alpine grasses necessary to its existence.

C. lancifolia. Leaves and bracts lance-shaped. Tall, slender; stems solitary. Bracts and flowers crimson. Rare. Douglas Island.

C. lutescens. Stems 3–5 inches; bracts ovate and 3-cleft, yellow; tips often brown or red. Alpine meadows of the Interior.

C. pallida. "Pale Paintbrush." Height 12–18 inches. Leafy stems. Flower bracts greenish yellow. Occurs in meadows at high altitudes and also at sea level. Often grows along roadsides with various weeds. All of Southeastern Alaska and rarely in the Interior. (Illus. p. 26.)

C. parviflora. With brilliant red bracts. Found from Skagway southward. (Illus. p. 27.)

C. tristis. Small, with red bracts. Circle and other parts of the Interior; rarely at high altitudes in Southeastern Alaska.

CERASTIUM (Greek for "horn," alluding to the shape of the seed pod, which suggests a powder horn). Caryophyllaceae. "Mouse-Eared Chickweed."

C. alpinum. A profuse-blooming, attractive plant, with flowers larger than the type. Found in many parts of the Interior. (Illus. p. 27.)

C. arvense. A dense-growing, trailing plant, its leaves and stems covered with sticky hairs. Numerous, small, white flowers with 5-cleft petals. Considered a troublesome weed by gardeners.

C. Fischerianum. Also a common form.

CHAMAEDAPHNE (*chamai,* "dwarf," and *daphne,* the "laurel," in ancient Greek, alluding to its dwarf habit and evergreen leaves). Ericaceae.

C. calyculata. "Leather Leaf." Bush with spreading horizontal branches. From 1 to 3 feet. Leaves oblong, short-petioled, and curled at the margins; dull green above, rusty beneath. Small, white, nodding, bell-shaped flowers. Common in the Interior.

Clintonia uniflora
Cochlearia oblongifolia

Coptis asplenifolia
Coptis trifolia

· 35

CHAMAECYPARIS.

C. nootkatensis. "Yellow Alaska Cedar." Distributed along the coast south from Sitka. Has ascending branches, tremulous at the extremities; branchlets flattened; dark cones ½ inch in diameter, round and hard. Attains considerable height. Its aromatic yellow wood has many uses, including furniture-making.

CHRYSANTHEMUM (Greek, "golden flower"). Compositae.

C. arcticum. The "Ox-Eye Daisy" of the North. Selects its dwelling place along the beaches and salt marshes, at times covered with salt water. Yellow disk with thick, white rays on stems 8–12 inches, above a clump of dark-green, somewhat fleshy foliage. Flowers showy, often two inches across. All along the coast. (Illus. p. 30.)

CICUTA (old name of "Hemlock"). Umbelliferae. Large bog plants with coarse, much-divided foliage, somewhat resembling Angelica. Small, white flowers in large umbels.

C. Douglasii. "Water Hemlock," "Poison Parsnip." Probably all species are poisonous, and *C. Douglasii* is extremely so. Common from Skagway southward. (Illus. p. 30.)

C. occidentalis is the Interior species, similar in appearance to the preceding.

C. vagans is more slender. Interior.

CLADOTHAMNUS (Greek, *klados,* "branch," and *thamnus,* "bush"). Ericaceae.

C. pyrolaeflorus. Deciduous shrub, with much the appearance of an Azalea, 4–10 feet. Grows in exposed locations on mountain tops, where the whole plant is almost prostrate on account of the weight of snow which covers it the greater part of the time. Leaves lance-shaped, 1–2 inches long, pale green. Flowers solitary; corolla divided nearly to base into five oblong petals. The pinkish copper color of the flowers suggests the common name of "Copper Bush." Southeastern Alaska. (Illus. p. 31.)

CLAYTONIA (after John Clayton of Virginia, one of the earliest American botanists). Portulacaceae. "Spring Beauty." Small, smooth, succulent, perennial herbs.

C. parviflora. Pink flowers in clusters at the end of the long lax stems. Parts of Southeastern Alaska.

C. siberica. White or rose-colored flowers; sprawling, fleshy stems. Plant often attains a spread of 18 inches in moist, rich soil. Flowers star-shaped, with five petals and five stamens, in racemes springing from the axils of the leaves. One of the first spring flowers to appear, persisting all summer. (Illus. p. 31.)

C. tuberosa. From a bulb. Slender stalk about 8 inches long; two lance-shaped leaves halfway, terminating in a panicle of four-petaled, white flowers. Bulb is used by Indians for food. Interior.

CLINTONIA (after De Witt Clinton, the famous Governor of New York, promoter of the Erie Canal). Liliaceae.

C. uniflora. "Queen's Cup," "Blue Bead." Low-growing plant with broad, shining leaves; showy, white, 6-petaled flowers; rarely two on a stem; followed by blue berries. Grows in cool, moist leaf mold. Occurs only in southern part of the Territory. (Illus. p. 34.)

COCHLEARIA (Greek, *cochlear,* a "spoon," referring to the leaves). Cruciferae.

C. oblongifolia. Small, tufted, fleshy seaside herb, covered with a profusion of small, white flowers. Found among rocks along the beach of the entire Alaska coast. (Illus. p. 34.)

Corallorhiza inata
Cornus instolonea

Cornus canadensis
Cornus canadensis (fruit)

COMANDRA (name alludes to the hairs in the flowers). Santalaceae. More or less parasitically attached to the roots of other plants.

C. livida. "Timberberry." Small, smooth, perennial herb of the Interior. Grows in open dry places. Alternate leaves thin, oblong, almost sessile. Inconspicuous flowers sparingly in axils of leaves. Petals wanting; stamens same in number as 4–5-cleft calyx lobes. Followed by bright orange, drupe-like fruit.

COMARUM (an old Greek name). Rosaceae.

C. palustre. "Marsh Cinquefoil." This species is allied to Potentilla, which it resembles, but differs in having the lateral style unknown in Potentilla. Eight inches to one foot; pinnate leaves and solitary, purple flowers. Petals shorter than the calyx lobes. Fruit resembles the strawberry but is spongy instead of juicy. Grows in wet meadows in all parts of Alaska.

COELOPLEURUM. Umbelliferae. Stout, glabrous perennials, with large, 2–3-times ternate leaves. Closely related to Angelica, Heracleum, and Cicuta.

C. Omlini. Juneau to the Interior.

COPTIS (Greek, "cut," from the cut leaves). Ranunculaceae. "Gold Thread." Low, stemless plants, with slender rootstocks. The bitter roots yield a tonic medicine known as "Gold Thread," also a yellow dye.

C. asplenifolia. Has beautiful, shining, fern-like evergreen foliage; inconspicuous yellow flowers. Grows in leaf mold and shade. Southeastern Alaska. (Illus. p. 35.)

C. trifolia. Has compound, 3-parted leaves. Flowers showy, white, star-shaped. Southeastern Alaska. (Illus. p. 35.)

CORALLORHIZA (Greek for "coral root"). Orchidaceae. "Coral Root." Low-growing orchids, growing in woods. Parasitic on roots and destitute of green foliage. Flowers small, somewhat two-lipped, usually spurred at the base. Roots are branched exactly like coral. Both of the following species are common in Southeastern Alaska.

C. inata. Smaller than *C. Mertensiana.* Stem and flowers greenish yellow. (Illus. p. 38.)

C. Mertensiana. Scape many-flowered and vigorous. Stem and flowers purplish.

CORNUS (ancient Latin name). "Dogwood." Of the dwarf herbaceous forms, two are native Alaskans. Both are creeping ramblers with woody rootstocks and oval, pointed leaves. In common with all Dogwoods, the flowers are gathered into a dense head, enclosed in a large collar formed by four white bracts. This is followed by a cluster of red berries.

C. canadensis is the most common of the two trailers. Extends over most of the Territory. Its flowers are greenish. Its leaves form a whorl below the flower and there is usually a pair near the middle of the stem. (Illus. p. 39.)

C. instolonea. "Red Osier Dogwood." Shrub to 10 feet, with dark red branches and prostrate stem. Inconspicuous flowers in dense cymes, 2–3 inches wide. Fruit white, showy. Circle southward. (Illus. p. 38.)

C. unalaschensis has smaller and more narrowly pointed flower bracts. Its flowers are purplish-black. Distinguished from *C. canadensis* by its branching stem and lighter-green leaves. Blooms earlier and the berries are larger. Rare in Southeastern Alaska and particularly common in the Aleutian Islands.

CORYDALIS (Greek name for the "Crested Lark"). Fumariaceae. Hardy plants allied to the Dutchman's Breeches, except that the Dutchman's Breeches has two spurs and Corydalis one. "Wild Bleeding Heart."

C. aurea. More or less decumbent. Foliage finely dissected. Flowers pale yellow; pods pendulous. Open places in the Interior.

Cryptogramma acrostichoides
Dianthus repens

Dodecatheon pauciflorum
Draba nivalis

43

C. pauciflora. About 6 inches tall. Leaves palmate at end of slender stem; succulent and frail. Flowers lavender, spurred, in close clusters at end of stem. Interior.

C. sempervirens. Erect branching stems, 1–1½ feet in height. Large, compound, glaucous foliage, deeply lobed. Flowers in racemes, spurred, rose-shaded lavender, tipped with yellow. Seed pods erect. Rocky places and clearings of the Interior.

CRYPTOGRAMMA (Greek, "a concealed line," referring to the submarginal sori). Polypodiaceae. Hardy subalpine ferns.

C. acrostichoides. "Rock Brake." Height about 8 inches. Leaves of two sorts: the fertile leaves contracted, and the sori covered by the infolded margin of the segments, forming podlike bodies. Among rocks. Southeastern and Southwestern Alaska. (Illus. p. 42.)

CYPRIPEDIUM ("Venus' slipper"). Orchidaceae. "Lady's Slipper," "Moccasin Flower."

C. guttatum. Two leaves; flowers produced singly; pink blotched with purple. Wooded hillsides, Circle, Kodiak.

C. passerimum. Stems about 8 inches; leaves oval to lanceolate. Flowers solitary, white or pale magenta, spotted with deep magenta. Wet or open woods. Northern Interior.

DELPHINIUM (Greek, "a dolphin," from the resemblance of the flower). Ranunculaceae. "Larkspur."

D. Brownii. A strong-growing plant, 3–4 feet, having all the characteristics of the garden varieties, which are too well known to require description. Flowers very dark blue. Common from Cordova northward.

An undetermined, dwarf alpine species is found in the extreme north.

DIANTHUS (Greek for "Jove's flower"). Caryophyllaceae. "Pink." Mostly perennials, forming tufts, with grasslike leaves.

D. repens. The only Dianthus known to be indigenous to Alaska. Plant very small and tufted, the one-flowered, slender stems rarely reaching more than 3–4 inches. Flowers relatively large, purplish-rose, odorless. Grows on rocky cliffs and in exposed locations only in the Interior. (Illus. p. 42.)

DIAPENSIA (ancient name of obscure application). Diapensiaceae.

D. lapponica. Forms compact, dense, cushion-like tufts, woody. Evergreen foliage very small and thick. Flowers ½ inch to 1 inch in diameter, 5-petaled, bell-shaped, cream-flushed rose. Flower stems become 1–2 inches long. Plentiful on high mountain tops of the Interior.

DODECATHEON (Greek, "twelve gods"; old name having no application here). Primulaceae. Small perennial herbs, with a basal tuft of thick leaves and flowers in an umbel on a naked scape. Corolla lobes and calyx sharply reflexed, the long slender anthers converging into a cone. All species have a yellow circle at the base of the corolla. The common name, "Shooting Star," is very applicable, as the sharp point formed by the connivant anthers seems to be shooting ahead and the reflexed corolla falls behind like the tail of a comet. The flowers, although facing downward, do not droop in humility but are very alert in appearance; and the sharp dart, poised for striking, suggests another common name, "Bird's Bill." The marked similarity of the flowers in all Alaska species makes the genus easy of identification.

D. integrifolium. A strong-growing species occurring in the southern part of the Territory.

D. Jeffreyii. Common near Matanuska, and also found in Southeastern Alaska, where it grows in damp meadows.

Dryas Drummondii
Dryopteris diliata

Echinopanax horridum
Empetrum nigrum

47

D. pauciflorum. Leaves petiolate. Smaller than other species. Found on hillsides and cliffs around Juneau. (Illus. p. 43.)

DRABA (Greek name for "a cress"). Cruciferae. "Whitlow Grass." A large genus of small alpines, many of which are inconspicuous weeds.

D. aleutica. Distinctive species found around Seward and on the Aleutians. Almost stemless tuft of mossy foliage. Long, single root. Small, white flowers.

D. nivalis. A biennial with showy, deep-yellow, 4-petaled blossoms, in racemes. Slender gray leaves, small and numerous, tufted. Grows among rocks and is plentiful in the Interior. (Illus. p. 43.)

DROSERA (Greek *droseros,* dewy, from the dew-like excretions on the tips of the leaf hairs). Droseraceae. "Sundew." A genus of small insectivorous herbs.

D. longifolia. Similar to *D. rotundifolia,* except that the leaves are elongated. Southeastern Alaska.

D. rotundifolia. Grows in very wet moss of the muskeg swamps. Odd little plant, consisting of a rosette of fleshy leaves covered with hairs that secrete a viscid fluid which entangles and catches insects. Leaves round, with long, non-glandular petiole. Flower scape slender, ending in cymes of white or pink bloom. Southeastern Alaska.

DRYAS (Greek, "wood nymph"). Rosaceae. Dwarf hardy evergreen, somewhat shrubby plants. Leaves whitish beneath. Growing in exposed locations where there is considerable moisture. One of the most attractive characteristics is the persistent style which elongates with age and forms a fluffy plume. All of the following are found in Mount McKinley Park and in most of the Interior and the Southwestern section. *D. Drummondii* is found as far south as Sitka.

D. Drummondii. Densely growing, with oak-shaped leaves; flowers yellow, with 6 petals, and never widely open. The blossoms of this species are followed by beautiful feathery styles. (Illus. p. 46.)

D. integrifolia. The rarest of the Alaska species. Flowers are creamy white. Surface of the leaves is smooth, and edges are not toothed or lobed.

D. octopetala. This beautiful species is offered by many commercial growers. Creamy-white flowers, with 8 petals, one inch or more across. Very floriferous. Forms dense mats. Foliage oak-shaped, smaller than that of *D. Drummondii.*

DRYOPTERIS (Greek, "oak fern"). Polypodiaceae. "Wood fern."

D. diliata. One of the most beautiful of Alaska ferns. One to three feet. Stalk naked about halfway. Tri-pinnate leaves of yellowish green. Grows from a crown usually in shade. Not evergreen. Very graceful. Southeastern Alaska. (Illus. p. 46.)

D. fragrans. "Fragrant fern." Small alpine among rocks of the Interior.

ECHINOPANAX (Greek, "hedgehog," referring to the prickly nature of the plant).

E. horridum. "Devil's Club." A tall, deciduous shrub, well known in the southern portion of the Territory. All parts of the plant are densely prickly, and it is a menace to those traveling through unbroken country where it abounds. The large leaves of tropical aspect and clusters of red berries render it a very handsome plant. (Illus. p. 47.)

ELAEAGNUS (ancient Greek name, meaning a kind of willow; from *elaios*, "olive"). Elaeagnaceae.

E. argentea. "Silverberry." Erect, very ornamental shrub, sometimes attaining 6 feet. Spineless, stoloniferous, with red-

Epilobium anagallidifolium
Epilobium angustifolium

Epilobium latifolium
Epilobium luteum

dish-brown branches. Leaves oval, silvery on both sides, 1–3 inches long. One to three bell-shaped flowers in clusters growing from axils of leaves; white, yellow within; followed by small oval fruit, densely clothed with silver scales. Interior.

EMPETRUM (Greek, *em*, "in," *petros*, "rock"; often growing in rocks). Ericaceae. Creeping evergreen shrub, densely branched, with small crowded leaves.

E. nigrum. "Crowberry." Flowers inconspicuous; black fruit profusely borne. Common all along the coast, where it climbs from moist shady woods at sea level to the edge of eternal snows. (Illus. p. 47.)

EPILOBIUM (Greek, "upon the pod," referring to the structure of the flower). A number of species are indigenous to Alaska, both annual and perennial, most of which are undesirable weeds. The perennial species mentioned here have claim to considerable beauty.

E. anagallidifolium. A tiny dwarf, its clustered growth covered in early spring with pinkish-lavender flowers. Found usually at high altitudes. Southeastern Alaska. (Illus. p. 50.)

E. angustifolium. Old name of "Willow Herb," suggested by the willow-shaped leaves. It is commonly called "Fireweed" because it is usually the first plant to take possession of burned-over areas, quickly covering the blackened scars. Bold and striking, with strong invading underground rootstocks. Often attains 8 feet in height. Its bright, rose-magenta tint covers acres of waste space and is beautiful at a distance. (Illus. p. 50.)

E. latifolium. Not more than two feet in height at best. Dwarfed and flattened to the ground by the breath of glacier and the fierce winds at high altitude where it chooses its home. Its leaves are a luminous light green, and its very bright cerise blossoms are carried in loose panicles on densely branching stems. There is no place in Alaska where this and *E. angustifolium* are not found. (Illus. p. 51.)

E. luteum. A distinct species, 1 to 2 feet high, with dark green leaves and bell-shaped, yellow flowers. Occurs sparingly in Southeastern Alaska. (Illus. p. 51.)

EQUISETUM (from the Latin *equus,* "horse," and *seta,* "bristle"). Equisetaceae. This genus includes the weeds known as "Horsetail." They are flowerless plants, allied to ferns and club mosses. Several species appear in every part of Alaska.

ERIGERON (Greek, "old man of the spring," because of the hoariness of some species). Compositae. "Fleabane." Closely allied to the Aster.

E. acris and ***E. elongatus*** are tall, weedy roadside plants of the Interior. Panicles of small white flowers.

E. compositus. Tufted growth; fine dense foliage; white flowers on short stems.

E. lonchophyllus. About 6–10 inches high. Slender, lanceolate foliage; many stems from one crown; several white flowers at end of each stem. Grows in wet soil near Fairbanks.

E. peregrinum. Dotted over wide areas among the tall grasses in alpine meadows. Growing thus, the plant usually bears a solitary stem crowned with a single blossom, but when fortunate enough to find a place in the sun where it is not shouldered by coarse vegetation it makes a strong sturdy growth with several flower stems. Pink flowers, deepening with age. (Illus. p. 54.)

E. Turneri. Thickly branching from the crown. Numerous lavender flowers, with yellow center about 1 inch across. Dry roadsides. Circle, south to McCarthy.

E. unalaschensis. Very dwarf, with pinkish-white flowers on short fuzzy stems. Southwestern and Southeastern Alaska. (Illus. p. 54.)

E. uniflorus. Tufted, fine dense foliage. Flowers white. Whole plant not over 3 inches. High alpine near Summit Glacier.

Erigeron peregrinum
Erigeron unalaschensis

Eriophorum angustifolium
Eriophorum Chamissonis

ERIOPHORUM (Greek, "wool-bearing"). Cyperaceae. "Alaska Cotton." Perennial, rushlike plants, bog-loving, 18 inches to 2 feet tall, with strongly spreading roots. Flowers in dense heads, the perianth bristles very numerous and elongated, producing a fluffy ball of "cotton." Much used for winter house decoration. At the end of the blooming season the tufts of fiber, operating as parachutes, serve to distribute the seeds.

E. alpinum. Tiny. Many stems springing from one crown, each bearing a small white head.

E. angustifolium. Each stalk bears several silky white heads. Southwestern and Southeastern Alaska. (Illus. p. 55.)

E. Chamissonis. Single head of a lovely beige color. A very strong-growing species. Covers wide areas of meadow land near Juneau. (Illus. p. 55.)

E. gracile. Similar to *E. angustifolium* but smaller. Interior.

E. opacum. Heads silky and close, not fluffy. Tall, slender, forming large "niggerheads" over swamps of parts of the Interior.

E. polystachion. Tall, heavy stem. Several heads to stalk. Interior.

E. Scheuchzeri. Similar to *E. Chamissonis,* but the heads are pure white. Grows profusely near Juneau.

E. vaginatum. Vigorous. Forms immense "niggerheads," sometimes standing 2 or 3 feet above the wet ground in which it grows. Interior. Single head to each stalk.

ERITRICHIUM. Boraginaceae. The gem of all the high alpine treasures. The cerulean-blue flower, of much the aspect of the Forget-me-not, is almost destitute of stem, covering the dense tuft of furry leaves in such a manner that the foliage is hardly visible through the azure veil. There have been reported one species growing on rocky cliffs at high altitudes on

Eagle Summit and on the Pribilof Islands; another species at Goodnews Bay, where it is locally known as the "Platinum Flower" because a rich vein of that precious metal has been discovered in the mountain on whose top it grows; and a rather large species near Healy. The identity of these species is as yet undetermined.

FILIX. Polypodiaceae. Ferns with pinnately compound fronds of thin texture. Creeping rhizomes.

F. fragile. Small, fragile. Foliage along three-fourths of the stem. Southeastern Alaska and in the Interior.

F. montana. Very slender little fern, with long naked stipe and plume of delicate foliage. Growing among rocks in the Interior.

FRAGARIA (Latin, "fragrance," from the smell of the fruit). Rosaceae. "Strawberry."

F. chiloensis. The probable origin of the ordinary cultivated strawberries of America. Found almost exclusively along beaches just beyond high-water mark. This species in various forms extends from western Alaska to southern Chile.
In the Interior we have *F. yukonensis,* which produces small roundish berries.

FRITILLARIA (Latin, *fritillus,* commonly understood to be a "checkerboard," from the tessellated or checkered flowers of some species). Liliaceae. Bulbous plants, closely resembling the Lily.

F. camschatcensis (the original spelling, but often variously misspelled): "Squaw Lily," "Rice Root," and "Indian Rice" are some of its many vernacular names, suggested by the fact that where it grows in abundance it is a common article of food among the Indians; there are many instances of persons having subsisted on the bulbs for a long time when other food was scarce. The bulbs are eaten boiled, and also from the dried

Fritillaria camschatcensis
Galium boreale

58

Gentiana Douglasiana
Gentiana platypetala

59

bulbs is produced a flour which is made into cakes, cooked, and eaten as bread. The conical-shaped bulb is entirely covered with numerous bulblets, the whole resembling a cluster of boiled rice. The nodding, very dark purplish-maroon bells are divided into six segments and lack the characteristic checkering. From one to four are produced at the top of the sturdy 8- to 12-inch stem. Their disagreeable odor renders them unattractive as cut flowers. Interesting sights to the tourists visiting Southeastern Alaska are the acres of marshland covered with this plant. It also climbs to considerable heights. This is a native of Siberia, whence it has wandered down the entire coast of Alaska. (Illus. p. 58.)

GALIUM (Galion was the name of a plant mentioned by Dioscorides as used in curdling milk; *G. vernum* is used abroad for this purpose). Rubiaceae. "Bedstraw" or "Ladies' Bedstraw," so called because of the legend that one of these plants was in the hay on which the mother of Jesus rested. Characterized by its mathematical habit due to the whorled leaves.

G. aparine. Very lax stems with almost the aspect of a vine. Tiny flowers springing from the axils of whorled leaves. Aleutian Islands and Southeastern Alaska.

G. boreale. Perennial, stoloniferous, forming patches. Stems smooth, 1 to 3 feet high, erect. Large fluffy panicles of very small white flowers, useful in bouquets for lightening heavier flowers. All over northern part of the Territory. (Illus. p. 58.)

G. columbianum. A fragile little plant, with trailing stems. Pribilof Islands, Interior, and Southeastern Alaska.

G. trifidum. Not easily distinguished from above. Wet places of the Interior.

G. trifolium. Lax, vinelike stems. Small white flowers in threes on a slender inch-long stem from each whorl of leaves. Interior, Aleutian Islands, and Southeastern Alaska.

GAULTHERIA (named by Kalm after Dr. "Gaulthier," a physician in Quebec, whose name was really written Gaultier). Ericaceae.

G. Shallon. "Salal." Low shrub, to 2 feet, with spreading glandular branches; leaves round or oval, thick and evergreen. Pinkish flowers nodding in terminal and axillary racemes, followed by purplish-black fruit, glandular, hairy. Extreme southern part of Alaska.

GENTIANA (after Gentius, King of Illyria, who is said to have discovered the medicinal value of these plants; the plant which he knew was probably *G. lutea,* the root of which furnishes the gentian of drugstores). Gentianaceae. Among the most desirable of alpine plants and generally of blue flowers.

G. acuta. Attains about 8 inches. Flowers dark blue, both axillary and terminal. Upright and branching. Leaves small and shining. Interior, and Southeastern Alaska.

G. algida (also *G. Romanzovii*). A distinctive species; very dwarf. Stout short stems. Abundant, lance-shaped leaves. Several blue flowers at end of stem. Shumagin Islands. False Pass.

G. americana. Tiny, fragile plants with opposite leaves. Terminal purple blossom. Interior, usually on mountain summits.

G. Douglasiana. Grows through moss in muskeg swamps. Flowers white, wide open, starlike, with five petals and five shorter sepals, both axillary and terminal. Leaves few, small, shiny, and opposite. Upright and branching. In late summer certain muskeg swamps around Juneau are white with this little plant. (Illus. p. 59.)

G. glauca. Found at very high altitudes, this rare alpine seeks a moist position near an alpine lake or stream. Tufted, with many branches from the same root; leaves small, glistening, in little whorled rosettes along the short stem. Flowers a peculiar greenish-blue, which never open, borne in clusters at the top of the stem. Interesting but not showy. Juneau, Nome, Kenai Mountains.

Geranium erianthum
Geum calthifolium

Harrimanella Stellariana
Heracleum lanatum

63

G. platypetala. Vigorous plant with fleshy opposite leaves set thickly along the 8–12-inch stems; root branching. Very strong root, which intertwines among the rocks in its chosen habitat at high altitudes. Strikingly blue, 4-lobed flowers, borne singly, or rarely in clusters, at the top of the stem. Only the strongest sunlight induces the tightly furled globes partially to open. The most beautiful of the Alaskan gentians. Profuse in Southeastern Alaska, Nome, and parts of the Interior. (Illus. p. 59.)

G. propinqua. Attains about 8 inches. Not root-branching. Manner of growth like *G. Douglasiana,* but its home is less moist. Flowers very dark purple. Has a wide range over most of the Interior and Southeastern Alaska.

GERANIUM (Greek, "crane," from the resemblance of the fruit to a crane's bill). Geraniaceae. Common name, "Crane's Bill."

G. Bicknellii. A weed of the interior.

G. erianthum. A vigorous and showy plant 18 inches to 2 feet tall. Flowers 5-petaled, about 1½ inches across, of a pleasing shade of blue, darkly veined, and borne in loose panicles at the top of the branching, leafy stems. Occasionally an albino form is encountered. Leaves much-lobed. The seeds, when ripened, separate themselves from the ovary and curl up. Grows in moist woods and also above timber line in alpine meadows. Has a wide range over most of the Territory. (Illus. p. 62.)

G. Richardsonii. Stems solitary or several, leafless to the inflorescence. Sometimes 3 feet tall. Flowers white or heliotrope. Sitka.

GEUM (probably originally from the Greek, *geuo,* to have a taste; referring to the roots). Rosaceae. "Avens." Herbs with perennial rhizome; root leaves crowded, the alternate lobes often smaller, the terminal one largest. Stem leaves few and bractlike. The several species indigenous to Alaska have little claim to beauty except the following:

64

G. calthifolium. The name is descriptive of the rounded terminal leaf lobes, which resemble those of Caltha but are hairy above and below. Showy, brilliant, yellow blossoms, 1–2 inches across; five round petals. Calyx is persistent; seeds have feathery styles. Alpine meadows, Southeastern Alaska. (Illus. p. 62.)

G. macrophyllum. A common weed of roadsides and waste places. Flowers small, but the characteristic bright yellow; leaves large and hairy. The plant is more attractive after the flowers are gone and it has produced its seeds in round spiny heads. Over most of the Territory.

G. Rossii. Flowers like *G. calthifolium*, but delicate pinnate leaves, deeply lobed. An alpine of the Interior.

HABENARIA (Greek, a "rein" or "strap," referring to the shape of parts of the flower). Orchidaceae. "Rein Orchis."

H. orbiculata. Leaves round, lying on the ground. Flowers numerous, loosely clustered, greenish; lip white. Flower spike about 6 inches long. Growing in bogs of various parts of southern Alaska and the Interior.

HARRIMANELLA (named for Edward Henry Harriman of the Harriman Expedition). Ericaceae. Formerly included in the Cassiope genus, which it resembles; but the flower cups have straight edges instead of recurved and the foliage is thick and soft instead of scalelike.

H. Stellariana. A beautiful small member of the heath family, which grows on the mountain tops of the Coast region. (Illus. p. 63.)

HEDYSARUM (Greek for "sweet smell"). Leguminosae.

H. americanum. Perennial herb with pinnate leaves and racemes of violet, pealike blossoms. Alpine. Sometimes attains 2½ feet. The root in summer is hard and woody but in winter becomes soft and is eaten by the Indians like carrots. Common in the Interior.

Heuchera glabra
Impatiens occidentalis

Iris setosa
Kalmia microphylla

67

HERACLEUM (dedicated to Hercules, who used it in medicine, according to Pliny). Umbelliferae.

H. lanatum. "Cow Parsnip," "Indian Rhubarb," and "Wild Celery" are some of the vernacular names for this bold plant, which is very conspicuous in the wild growth all over Alaska. Tall and coarse, sometimes attaining 10 feet in moist deep soil. Leaves deeply lobed. Flowers white, in umbels often as large as a dinner plate. When bruised emits a disagreeable pungent odor. Dried stalks and skeleton flower clusters remain after the plant dies down in winter, and are really beautiful after a heavy fall of snow. Each dried pedicel holds a collection of snowflakes, and the plant appears to bloom again. (Illus. p. 63.)

HEUCHERA (after Johann Heinrich von Heucher, 1677–1747, Professor of Botany at Wittenberg). Saxifragaceae. "Alum Root." Herb with tuft of heart-shaped leaves, from which spring many slender scapes a foot or more in height and bearing panicles of small flowers.

H. glabra. Shining leathery foliage, which is beautifully colored in autumn. Flowers greenish white, inconspicuous, but producing a dainty, airy effect, and useful in cut-flower arrangements. Likes best a home in crevices of rocks. Southwestern and Southeastern Alaska. (Illus. p. 66.)

HIERACIUM (Greek, "a hawk"; it is said that ancients believed that hawks sharpened their eyesight by using the sap of these plants). Compositae. "Hawkweed."

H. albiflorum. Upper part of stem smooth, but hairy at the base. From 8 to 18 inches in height. White-flowered.

H. gracile. Slender, dwarf plant. Leaves smooth, long-petioled, spoon-shaped. Flower heads black, hairy. Flowers pale yellow, of somewhat the aspect of a Dandelion.

H. triste. A tufted plant. Numerous slender stems rising from the basal clump of spatulate leaves, bearing pale-yellow flower heads, several to each stem, with woolly involucre. Most showy of Alaska species. Exposed heights near Skagway.

HIPPURIS ("horsetail," from the looks of the plant). Haloragidaceae. All of the following occur in Southeastern Alaska.

H. montana. A tiny form of *H. tetraphylla.*

H. tetraphylla. Distinguished from *H. vulgaris* by four leaves in whorls. Large.

H. vulgaris. The commonest of the Alaska species. Grows in deep water, with the shoots standing above the water. Leaves very small, 6 to 12 in crowded whorls along the stem. Flowers small and inconspicuous; sessile in the axils.

IMPATIENS (Latin, having reference to the pods, which, when ripe, on slight pressure burst open, scattering the seed). Balsaminaceae. "Touch-me-not," "Jewelweed."

I. occidentalis. Very tender, succulent annual. Common in Southeastern Alaska and westward. Grows in moist waste places and along roadsides. Leaves smooth, broadly lance-shaped. Yellow-lipped flowers, with long incurving spur, sparsely dotted with brown. (Illus. p. 66.)

IRIS (Greek, "rainbow"). Widely distributed genus of perennial herbs, too well known to require description.

I. setosa. This is truly the Alaska Iris, as it occurs freely throughout the Coast region from Nome to Ketchikan, spreading over acres of marshland, and producing a wonderful expanse of blue. Flowers purple-blue, usually of a very dark shade, but occasionally pale lavender and intermediate shades; rarely pure white. Vigorous plants, with strong, sword-like foliage, about 2 feet in height. (Illus. p. 67.)

JUNIPERUS (ancient Latin name). Pinaceae. "Juniper."

J. horizontalis. A more ornamental plant than the next species. Long, trailing branches, with numerous short branchlets. Scale-like foliage and a profusion of black fruit with so much bloom as to appear light blue. Interior.

Lathyrus maritima
Ledum groenlandicum

Ligusticum Hultenii
Limnorchis leucostachys

Linnaea americana
Listera nephrophylla

J. sibericus, var. *nana.* Evergreen shrub, with needle leaves. Black berries with bloom. Entire plant has a silvery appearance. Not over 2 feet, procumbent. Particularly plentiful around Petersburg, where it grows in muskegs. Also found in other parts of Southeastern Alaska.

KALMIA (after Peter Kalm, Swedish botanist). Ericaceae. Ornamental shrubs. "Bog Laurel."

K. microphylla. Dwarf, creeping, evergreen shrub, with inconspicuous leaves and showy, rose-colored blossoms in large terminal umbels. Single blossoms are exquisitely symmetrical. Grows in bogs of Southeastern Alaska. (Illus. p. 67.)

KRUHSIA streptopoides. Classed sometimes as a dwarf Streptopus. Not over 6 inches tall. Broad leaves; flowers deep wine-colored, with green tips. Fruit, round red berry. Shady woods in Southeastern Alaska.

LARIX (ancient Latin name). Pinaceae. "Larch," "Tamarack."

L. laricina. A deciduous coniferous tree, with attractive, whorled leaves. Regular pyramidal habit. Wet places of the Interior.

LATHYRUS (name used by Theophrastus for some leguminous plant). Leguminosae.

L. maritima. "Beach Pea." Stout stems, 1–2 feet long, angled, decumbent. Leaves thick and glaucous, nearly blue. Flowers shaded purple and rose. Seed pods long and hairy. Common on gravelly beaches along entire coast. (Illus. p. 70.)

L. palustris. Foliage much more slender than *L. maritima* above, lance-shaped. Wet valleys of the Interior.

74

Loiseleuria procumbens
Luetkea pectinata

Lupinus nootkatensis
Lycopodium alpinum

75

LEDUM (Ledon, ancient Greek name of Cistus). Ericaceae.

L. groenlandicum. Leaves are said to have been used during the Revolutionary War as a substitute for tea. Hence the common name, "Labrador Tea." Dwarf, evergreen shrub, growing 1 to 2 feet tall, leaves dark green, shiny on top and tomentose beneath. Feathery clusters of small, creamy-white flowers. Growing in muskegs all over Southeastern Alaska and in parts of the Interior. (Illus. p. 70.)

L. decumbens. A smaller plant with slender leaves. Otherwise very similar to preceding one. Plentiful in northern sections. In McKinley Park and other places of the Interior both species grow.

LEPARGYRAEA canadensis. Elaeagnaceae. "Soapolallie" is the Indian name for the berries borne by these medium-sized shrubs. Also known as "Soapberry," because the berries when beaten in water give rise to a froth resembling soapsuds. Leaves covered with stellate hairs; deciduous. Red berries. Interior.

LEPTARRHENA (name refers to slender or thin anthers). Saxifragaceae. Single species.

L. pyrolifolia. "Pear Leaf." Leaves leathery, evergreen, toothed, narrow at base. Flowers small, white, in bracted panicles. Southeastern Alaska.

LIGUSTICUM (Latin, referring to the ancient province of Liguria). Umbelliferae. "Lovage." Aquatics or bog plants, with aromatic roots and large, compound leaves.

L. Hultenii. An attractive plant, attaining under favorably wet conditions a height of 12 to 18 inches. Small white flowers in symmetrical corymbs. Often found growing on cliffs near the seashore, where it seems to enjoy an occasional shower bath from the spray. All along coast. (Illus. p. 71.)

LIMNORCHIS (from Greek, referring to marsh habitat). Orchidaceae. Terrestrial orchid.

L. borealis. Strong-growing, with tuberous roots. Flowers greenish-white at top of a thick, leafy stem. Occurs in swamps from Craig to Talkeetna.

L. dilitata. Slender form of *L. borealis.* Craig, Skagway.

L. graminifolia. A species with grassy foliage, found at Ketchikan.

L. leptoceratitis. Has long slender roots.

L. leucostachys. Tubers divided and somewhat palmate. Creamy-white flowers in a spike at the top of the thick stem, thrusting up through the rank vegetation of boggy flats. An enchanting perfume, which wins for it the nickname of "Wild Hyacinth." Southeastern Alaska. (Illus. p. 71.)

L. viridiflora. Green-flowered form. Tall slender growth. All along the coast.

LINNAEA (named after Linnaeus, at his own request; it was his favorite flower). Caprifoliaceae. "Twin Flower."

L. americana. Very similar to the European-introduced *Linnaea borealis.* Half-woody, creeping herb. Small, round, opposite leaves; evergreen. Flowers delicate, pink, nodding bells, in pairs, on slender, erect stems. Grows in leaf mold and shade; mildly fragrant. Entire Coast region and Interior. (Illus. p. 72.)

L. longiflora. Very similar to the preceding. Found growing in moss in deep woods at Mud Bay and near Craig.

LINUM (classical name). Linaceae. "Flax."

L. Lewisii. A species of the well-known cultivated Flax. One to two feet tall, of very slender growth. Large, lavender flowers, which open in the sun. In open meadows at Chitina and other parts of the Interior. Same manner of growth as the cultivated *L. alpina,* but taller.

Lycopodium annotinum
Lycopodium porophilum

Lysichitum americanum
Menyanthes trifoliata

79

LISTERA (after Martin Lister, English naturalist). Orchidaceae. "Tway Blade." Slender little plants bearing a pair of opposite leaves near the middle of the stem. Small, greenish flowers in a spike. Growing in leaf mold and moss in deep shade.

L. caurina, L. convallarioides, and *L. nephrophylla* (Illus. p. 72) are found in Alaska. Very similar, with slight structural differences.

LLOYDIA (after Edward Lloyd, who found one of the plants in Wales). Liliaceae. Small, bulbous plants related to Erythronium. Small bulb; slender stem. "Alp Lily."

L. serotina. Stem usually one-flowered, 3 to 5 inches tall. Flowers white, small, with dark stripe in center of each of the six petals. High altitudes. Southwestern and Southeastern Alaska.

LOISELEURIA (J. C. A. Loiseleur-Deslongchamps, physician and botanist of Paris). Ericaceae.

L. procumbens. "Mountain Azalea." Flat-growing, evergreen shrub, with very small, opposite, closely set leaves. Abundant, small, campanulate flowers of varying shades of rose, in terminal panicles. Rarely an albino form. Grows in meager soil on bare slopes at high altitudes. Also known as *Azalea procumbens.* Has a wide range over nearly all parts of the Territory. (Illus. p. 74.)

LOMARIA (Greek *loma,* "forage"). Polypodiaceae. Generic name for a group of ferns.

L. Spicant. "Deer Fern." Rhizome stout, somewhat woody; fronds attaining 18 inches; pinnae thick and numerous, with a hard, sword-like appearance, shorter near base. Common in Southeastern Alaska.

LONICERA (after Adam Lonicer, or Lonitzer, a German physician and naturalist). Caprifoliaceae. "Honeysuckle."

L. involucrata. "Black Twinberry." Shrub attaining 5 feet. Lance-shaped, pointed leaves. Flowers yellowish, slightly tinged red. Berries black, shining, almost enclosed by the large purple involucre. Southeastern Alaska.

LUETKEA (after Father Luetke, Russian sea captain, in charge of the fourth Russian voyage around the world). Rosaceae.

L. pectinata. Prostrate, creeping undershrub. Feathery evergreen trifid leaves of an unusual shade of green; ascending flower shoots 2–6 inches high, and small, creamy-white blossoms in upright racemes. Found usually at high altitudes, intertwined with the Cassiopes and *Vaccinium uliginosum.* Southeastern Alaska. (Illus. p. 74.)

LUPINUS (from the Latin *lupus,* "wolf," because a crop of Lupines was supposed to destroy fertility). Leguminosae.

L. arcticus. Similar to *L. nootkatensis,* except less robust. Fragrant. The Alaska Lupine of the Interior.

L. nootkatensis. Coarse, stocky herb. Downy leaves with several digitate leaflets. Papilionaceous flowers, shaded purplish-blue, tipped with white, in dense racemes. Grows in damp meadows, spreading over acres, and is common in Southwestern and Southeastern Alaska. (Illus. frontispiece, also p. 75.)

LYCOPODIUM (Greek, "wolf foot"). Lycopodiaceae. "Club Moss."

L. alpinum. Growing with Cassiopes and other alpine shrubs on mountain tops in Southeastern Alaska and, rarely, in the Interior. Scale-like leaves. (Illus. p. 75.)

L. annotinum. Long trailing branches, with silky leaves. Southeastern Alaska and Interior. (Illus. p. 78.)

L. clavatum. Another trailer, with branching stems. Southeastern Alaska, Interior, Aleutian Islands.

82

Menziesia ferruginea
Mertensia paniculata

Mimulus Langsdorfii
Mimulus Lewisii

L. complanatum. Scale-like foliage in bunches along the long stem. Southeastern Alaska and Interior.

L. inundatum. Wet situations, usually on the bank of a pond. Small, creeping. Southeastern Alaska.

L. obscurum. Handsomest of all the Alaska species. It is 6–12 inches high, forming a somewhat tree-like growth. Spikes erect. Found on Gravina Island and at Cleary Summit.

L. porophilum. Stem usually about 3 inches, often two-branched. Thickly disposed needle leaves. Grows in moss under trees. Southeastern Alaska. (Illus. p. 78.)

L. Selago. Small, erect. Dry alpine situations of the Interior.

L. sitchensis. An alpine form of Southeastern Alaska and the Interior.

LYSICHITON (Greek, "loose or free cloak," probably referring to the spathe). Also written Lysichitum. Araceae.

L. americanum. Very early in the spring, before the leaves, the large deep-yellow calla-like flowers appear. The leaves which follow, before the flower fades, attain in some cases a height of 5 feet. Its nickname of "Skunk Cabbage" is hardly deserved and has created considerable unjust prejudice against this truly handsome plant. While not particularly agreeable, its perfume is not at all insistent. Until recently this species was classed by American botanists as *L. camtschatcense*, which is quite a different plant. Southeastern Alaska. (Illus. p. 79.)

MALUS (Greek for "apple"). Rosaceae.

M. diversifolia. "Wild Crabapple." Tall shrub, stoloniferous; bears stout spines; white apple-blossoms and greenish fruit. Fairly common in Southeastern Alaska.

84

Moneses uniflora
Myosotis alpestris

85

Nephrophyllidium Crista-gallii
Nymphaea polysepala

Oxyria digyna
Oxytropis campestris

87

MENYANTHES (Greek, probably meaning "month flower"; perhaps because it flowers for about a month). Gentianaceae.

M. trifoliata. "Buck Bean." Grows in bogs and calm water, with creeping rootstock. Stalked, compound leaves, with three leaflets. White flowers, slightly tinted pink; the upper surface of the petals furry. (Illus. p. 79.)

MENZIESIA (after Archibald Menzies, surgeon and naturalist). Ericaceae. Allied to Rhododendron.

M. ferruginea. "False Azalea." One of the most beautiful shrubs of Southeastern Alaska. It can be recognized at a distance by its blue foliage, which grows in terminal clusters. Grows with blueberry as an undershrub in spruce and hemlock forests. Flowers bell-shaped on inch-long pedicles, in varying shades of coral pink. (Illus. p. 82.)

MERTENSIA (after Franz Carl Mertens, a German botanist). Boraginaceae. "Chiming Bells," "Lungwort."

M. maritima. (Also known as *Pneumaria maritima.*) A beach plant, with lax stems 1 foot or so long. Leaves fleshy, glaucous, margined red in late summer. Flowers small, blue. Along entire coast.

M. paniculata. Striking woodland plant with handsome hairy foliage; attains about 2 feet. Flowers bright blue, nodding bells; buds are pink. All over northern part of Territory. (Illus. p. 82.)

MIMULUS (Latin, "little mimic," from the grinning flowers). Scrophulariaceae. Vigorous herbs with showy flowers, shaped somewhat like those of the snapdragon. Sometimes called "Wild Snapdragon," "Monkey Flower."

M. Langsdorfii. Deep-yellow flowers, borne in great profusion; dark spots in throat. In moist places the plant attains a height of 2 feet or more. Often found growing in drainage ditches along roadsides where the impish faces grin up at the passer-by. Attractive to small insects. Coast region from Aleutian Islands south. (Illus. p. 83.)

M. Lewisii. Large flowers of a clear, rosy magenta, self-color. More often found in sandy, well-drained soil; but it is not particular as to the dampness of its situation. In great quantities in the neighborhood of Hyder. At higher altitudes than the preceding. (Illus. p. 83.)

MITELLA (diminutive of *mitra*, "a cap," applied to the form of the young pod). Saxifragaceae. "Mitrewort," "Bishop's Cap." Closely related to Tiarella.

M. pentandra. Leaves round, indistinctly lobed. Greenish flowers on slender, naked stems.

MONESES (Greek, "single delight"; from the pretty, solitary flower). Pyrolaceae. "One-flowered Pyrola," "Wood Nymph."

M. reticulata. Slightly different from *M. uniflora.* Has been found in the Prince William Sound section and at Strawberry Point on Lynn Canal.

M. uniflora. Leaves round, clustered at the base. Flowers single, drooping from top of slender scape 2–4 inches long, waxy white. Petals widely spreading; long pistil; anthers as in Pyrola but conspicuously 2-horned. Found in many parts of Alaska. (Illus. p. 85.)

MYOSOTIS (Greek, signifying "mouse ear," from the leaves). Boraginaceae. "Forget-me-not." Too well known to require description.

M. alpestris. The official Alaska territorial flower. Grows profusely all over the northern part of the Territory and as far south as Haines. Flowers large, and intensely blue, with yellow eye. Height of plant varies with altitude. On bleak mountain tops it is almost stemless and appears to be a very different plant from that of 18 inches in lower locations. (Illus. p. 85.)

Papaver pygmaeum
Papaver radicatum

Parnassia fimbriata
Parnassia Kotzebueii

91

MYRICA (ancient Greek name, possibly applied originally to the Tamarack). Myricaceae.

M. Gale (also *Gale palustris*). "Sweet Gale." Deciduous, aromatic shrub, with dark-brown branches, 1–5 feet. Fruit in small catkins with winged nutlets, crowded at end of last year's branches. Foliage densely growing. Grows in moist peaty soil from Ketchikan to Matanuska.

NEPHROPHYLLIDIUM. By some botanists not separated from Menyanthes. Gentianaceae.

N. Crista-gallii. "Deer Cabbage." Individual flowers larger than those of Menyanthes and not covered with fur. Leaves large, heavy and round, on stout stalks. Grows in muskeg pools and in hollows filled with melted snow on mountain tops. (Illus. p. 86.)

NYMPHAEA (from *Nympha* in Greek and Roman mythology, "a nature goddess"). Nymphaceae.

N. polysepala. "Alaska Water Lily." Springing from large rhizomes or rootstocks submerged in water. Leaves floating, sometimes a foot across. Flowers deep yellow, cup-like, with a pistillate knob in the center surrounded by numerous stamens. Attracts quantities of small insects. Coast region. (Illus. p. 86.)

OENANTHE (name refers to the vinous scent of the flowers). Umbelliferae.

O. sarmentosa. Large plant, closely related to Angelica; growing in wet situations. Hollow stems and large compound leaves; large umbel of small, white flowers. Southeast Alaska.

ONOCLEA (Greek, "closed vessel," alluding to the closely rolled sporophylls). Polypodiaceae.

O. Struthiopteris. Large fern, often growing shoulder-high. Fertile fronds erect, rigid, with contracted, berry-like divisions; sterile fronds taller than fertile. Creeping rootstock.

ORCHIS (Greek word referring to the shape of the tuberous roots of some species). Orchidaceae. The typical genus of the great family of Orchids.

O. rotundifolia. From palmate bulb. One oval leaf. Slender stem, about 4 inches. Flowers in spike at top of stem; pinkish or whitish; lip white, spotted with purple; pollen greenish. Swamps of the Interior.

OXYCOCCUS. Ericaceae. Fragile trailing shrub of muskeg swamps.

O. microcarpus. A smaller form than *O. oxycoccus;* of the Interior.

O. oxycoccus (also known as *Vaccinium oxycoccus*). "Cranberry." Tiny, pointed, evergreen leaves and pink blossoms, with reflexed petals. Red berry ¼ inch to ⅓ inch in diameter. Southeastern Alaska.

OXYRIA. Polygonaceae.

O. digyna. "Mountain Sorrel." A small Dock growing in wet alpine situations. Dwarf; leaves mostly basal. Flowers arranged in panicled racemes. Flower, fruit, and leaves shaded red. Wet alpine regions in all parts of the Territory. (Illus. p. 87.)

OXYTROPIS (Greek, "sharp keel"). Leguminoscae. "Locoweed." The genus is like Astragalus, but it is distinguished by a subulata beak at the tip of the keel.

O. campestris. Tufted; numerous lax stems from a thick rootstock; leaves pinnately compound, silvery-hairy; flowers pale yellow, pea-like. Plants a yard in diameter are not uncommon. Entire Coast region and Interior. (Illus. p. 87.)

O. deflexa. An Interior species.

O. Maydelliana. A dwarf alpine of the Interior.

94

Parnassia palustris
Pedicularis verticillata

Pentstemon sp.
Petasites hyperboreus

O. Mertensiana. Distinctive; leaves not pinnate; tufted; large, yellowish flowers. Eagle Summit.

O. nigrescens. Dwarf; calyx and flower stems covered with black hairs. Flowers purple. Northern Coast region.

PAPAVER (old Latin name). Papaveraceae. "Poppy."

P. pygmaeum. Tiny poppy, with pale pink or apricot flowers on 3-inch stems, from a small, close tuft of gray-green foliage. Reported at Point Hope, Goodnews Bay, and in the Kenai Lake region. In well-drained, rocky situations. (Illus. p. 90.)

P. radicatum. The Iceland Poppy of northern Alaska. Blossoms clear yellow; stems from 6 to 12 inches. Has a wide range, from the Arctic Circle and beyond, south as far as Cordova. (Illus. p. 90.)

PARNASSIA (after Mount Parnassus). Saxifragaceae. "Grass of Parnassus." Low-growing, moisture-loving, hardy perennial herbs, of tufted habit. Leaves petiolate and mostly basal, resembling those of the Violet. Small sessile scape leaf near middle of stem. Flowers white, veined with green. Five petals, five-parted calyx; fertile stamens five, alternating with petals.

P. fimbriata. Height 1 foot or less. Distinguished by petals being fringed near bottom. Showy. Southeastern Alaska. (Illus. p. 91.)

P. Kotzebueii. Much smaller than the preceding, in leaf, flower, and manner of growth, with flowers less attractive. Much-enlarged seed capsule surrounded by small, inconspicuous petals. Southeastern Alaska and Interior. (Illus. p. 91.)

P. palustris. Most vigorous species and the most common; found in many places in the Interior and along the entire Coast. The only species common in Europe, and the plant originally called "Grass of Parnassus." (Illus. p. 94.)

PARRYA (after Captain W. E. Parry, Arctic explorer). Cruciferae.

P. nudicaulis. "Parry's Wallflower." Raceme of large, lavender flowers, above close tuft of leaves. Thick root, somewhat woody. Alpine regions of Northern Coast and Interior.

PEDICULARIS (from Latin for "louse"; application not apparent). Scrophulariaceae. "Lousewort." Perennial herbs with finely cut foliage. Partially parasitic; probably require a particular host plant. Closely related to Castilleja, "Indian Paintbrush." Flowers borne in terminal, bracted spikes. Corolla two-lipped, the upper one with a long beak. Leaves much-divided, fern-like.

P. capitata. Yellow flowers in compact heads. Skagway to Interior.

P. labradorica. Yellow flowers. Occurs in swamps of the northern Coast and in the Interior.

P. lanata. Flowers bright magenta; spike very dense. Northern Coast region.

P. Oederi. About 6 inches tall; leaves glabrous; flowers yellowish, purple-tinted. Lower lip of corolla much shorter than upper. Interior, Southwestern, and Southeastern Alaska.

P. parviflora. Large; leaves glabrous, opposite. Flowers bright rose, in loose spikes or solitary in the axils. A seashore plant. Found near Valdez.

P. sudetica. Stems erect; leaves alternate. Flowers crimson-magenta. Large colonies found in moist woods at sea level. Southeastern Alaska and parts of the Interior.

P. verticillata. Stems lax. Leaves whorled. Flowers pale rose. Found at high altitudes among the grasses of alpine meadows. Southeastern Alaska and northern Coast region. (Illus. p. 94.)

97

Phyllodoce glanduliflora
Picea sitchensis

Pinguicula villosa
Pinguicula vulgaris

PENTSTEMON (Greek for "five stamens"; all five stamens being present, whereas related genera have only four; but in Pentstemon one of the stamens is sterile). Scrophulariaceae. "Beard Tongue." (Illus. p. 95.)

P. diffusus. A handsome plant, with characteristic tubular flowers in terminal racemes; reddish-purple, shaded magenta. Plant about one foot high; branches partly procumbent. Common near Hyder.

PERAMIUM ("through *amium,* 'love'," in allusion to medicinal properties). Orchidaceae. Sometimes included in the genus Goodyera. Conspicuous for their variegated foliage.

P. decipiens. "Rattlesnake Plantain." Inconspicuous, greenish flowers on a scape about 12 inches high. Foliage tufted; strongly edged and marked with white. Grows in moss and leaf mold under trees. Southeastern Alaska.

P. repens. Very similar to the preceding in appearance, but smaller. Interior.

PETASITES (Greek, "a broad-brimmed hat," referring to the large, broad leaves). Compositae. Large perennial herbs, with felty leaves. Coarse and weedy.

P. frigidus. Leaves slightly cleft, glabrous above and densely tomentose beneath. Flowers whitish with short rays, in a corymb at the top of a short scape before the leaves appear. Develops into a large plant often 3 feet tall. Above timber line. Coastal region.

P. hyperboreus (P. alaskansis). Somewhat the appearance of the preceding, but the leaves are deeply cleft. Flowers appear in late summer. Southeastern Alaska. (Illus. p. 95.)

P. sagittatus. Distinct. Huge, arrow-shaped, broad leaf, with shallow regular indentations. Interior.

PHYLLODOCE (after Phyllodoce, a sea nymph mentioned by Virgil). Ericaceae. "False Heather."

P. empetriformis. The Red Heather. The flowers are more open than those of the Yellow Heather described below, in clusters shaded from old rose to dark red. Interior.

P. glanduliflora. Prostrate, evergreen shrub with crowded leaves. A well-grown specimen covers several square feet. Flowers nodding, sulphur-yellow, borne profusely on slender pedicels in ascending terminal umbels. Found upon the exposed mountain slopes of Southwestern and Southeastern Alaska. Yellow Heather. (Illus. p. 98.)

PICEA (ancient Latin name derived from *pix*, "pitch"). Pinaceae. "Spruce." Handsome evergreen conifers, of regular pyramidal habit, with usually whorled spreading branches.

P. canadensis. "White Spruce" is the most valuable tree of the Interior, where it is used for lumber.

P. mariana. "Black Spruce" is a small scrubby species of Interior swamps.

P. sitchensis. "Sitka Spruce" is, next to Western Hemlock, the chief constituent of the coastal forests. It grows to large size and is the chief source of lumber in the Territory. It is our largest tree, and in favorable locations, trees 6 feet or more in diameter at waist height are not uncommon. (Illus. p. 98.)

PINGUICULA (diminutive of Latin *pinguis*, "fat," referring to the succulent and greasy foliage). Lentibulariaceae. "Butterwort." Small, carnivorous herbs with pretty, long-spurred flowers somewhat like a snapdragon, interesting because of their insectivorous habits. Grow in moist ground; fibrous roots; leaves in a basal rosette, broad and entire, yellowish-green, with odd transparency, soft, the upper surface covered with numerous glands secreting a digestive fluid, the margins infolding when an insect alights. Leaves disappear in winter and beneath the snow a fat nodule of greenish scales remains underground like a pseudo-bulb.

Pinus contorta
Pleurogyne rotata

Polemonium humile
Polemonium pulcherrimum

104

Polypodium occidentalis
Polystichum Braunii

P. villosa. A tiny species which grows in muskeg swamps. Flowers very dark blue. (Illus. p. 99.)

P. vulgaris. Flowers bright blue, rarely purple, with a darker throat lined with silk hairs. It is sometimes taken for a Violet by the unobserving. Southeastern Alaska and parts of the Interior. (Illus. p. 99.)

PINUS (ancient Latin name). Pinaceae.

P. contorta. "Lodgepole Pine." Grows to 20 feet. In youth quite symmetrical, but old trees are gnarled and picturesque. In muskeg swamps along the Coast and also on hillsides from Skagway to the Interior. (Illus. p. 102.)

PLEUROGYNE. Gentianaceae. "Marsh Felwort."

P. rotata. Dwarf plant, with much the appearance of a Gentian, growing in marshes throughout the Coast region. Five-lobed corolla, each lobe with two scales at the base. Flowers both terminal and axillary, dark blue or white. (Illus. p. 102.)

POLEMONIUM (ancient name, not explained; probably from the philosopher Poleman). Polemoniaceae. "Jacob's Ladder." "Greek Valerian."

P. acutifolium. A vigorous plant, attaining 2 feet or more. The characteristic foliage is strong and heavy. Dark blue flowers on stout stems. Along northern Coast and in many parts of the Interior.

P. humile. Small plant; erect stems 6–10 inches, growing out of the basal clump of fern-like leaves. Showy flowers, with yellow throat, ranging in color from very dark blue to pure white. All along the Coast. (Illus. p. 103.)

P. pulcherrimum. Very similar to *P. humile* except stronger-growing. Flowers large and showy, of a pretty, clear blue. Southwestern and Southeastern Alaska. (Illus. p. 103.)

105

Polystichum Lonchitis
Potentilla Anserina

Potentilla fruticosa
Potentilla villosa

107

POLYGONUM (Greek for "many-jointed"). Polygonaceae. "Jointweed," "Knotweed," "Smartweed."

P. Bistorta. One to two feet. Stems slender and wiry. Flowers bright pink, in a single, dense, oblong spike an inch or two long. Grows in damp meadows all along the Coast.

P. viviparum. Similar to the preceding except bulblet-bearing at base or throughout. Flowers white.

POLYPODIUM (Greek, "many feet," alluding to the extensive rootstocks). Polypodiaceae.

P. occidentalis. "Rock Fern," "Licorice Fern." Small, evergreen fern; fronds about 8 inches long; thick and stiff. On old logs and stumps and in thin leaf mold on boulders. Southwestern and Southeastern Alaska. (Illus. p. 104.)

POLYSTICHUM (Greek, "many rows," referring to the sori). Polypodiaceae.

P. Braunii. One of the most beautiful of the Southeastern Alaska ferns. Blades 18–24 inches long. Grows in the lightest of leaf mold, with the crown almost out of the ground. Covered with white down as it uncurls in spring. (Illus. p. 104.)

P. Lonchitis. Distinct. Leaves thick and rigid, with prickly margins, suggesting the name "Holly Fern." Southeastern Alaska. (Illus. p. 106.)

P. munitum. "Dagger Fern." Fronds often 3 feet. The large sword fern used by florists. Southeastern Alaska.

POPULUS (ancient Latin name, of disputed origin). Salicaceae. Soft-wooded trees of rapid growth. Broad-stalked leaves. Profusion of catkins, varying in different species. Resinous buds.

P. balsamifera. "Balsam Poplar." Common in the Interior.

P. candicans. The true "Balm of Gilead." The tree commonly called that in Southeastern Alaska is the Black Cottonwood, *P. trichocarpa* (see below).

P. tremuloides. "Aspen." Occasional tree of the Interior. White bark. Leaves on very slender, pliant petioles; tremble at the slightest breeze.

P. trichocarpa. "Black Cottonwood." Occurs in the river valleys along the Coast.

POTENTILLA (diminutive of Latin *potens,* "powerful"; referring to the medicinal properties). Rosaceae. "Cinquefoil," "Five-Finger."

Among the most showy of Alaska wild flowers. Some species, with showy yellow blossoms, may be found in every part of the Territory. Considerable confusion exists among some of the species where the difference is not noticeable and the plants vary only in a technical respect.

P. Anserina. A common beach plant all along the Coast. Its chief characteristic is the long red strawberry runners which are thrown out from the parent plant and form colonies. Leaves white beneath, pinnate—not the "five-finger" form of the type. (Illus. p. 106.) *P. pacifica* is very similar.

P. argentea. Like *Anserina,* but leaves decidedly silvery. River banks of the Interior.

P. biflora. A tufted alpine with finely dissected foliage. Interior.

P. fruticosa. Common at Nome and spreading over the entire Interior, but shuns the too-moist climate of the Panhandle. This is the only shrub of this numerous Alaska genus. Very floriferous and showy. Known in some localities as the "Tundra Rose," as it has somewhat the appearance of a small, single, yellow rose. (Illus. p. 107.)

P. uniflora. Very similar to *P. villosa.* Southeastern Alaska and Interior.

P. villosa. Dwarf plant, with beautiful iridescent foliage, densely silky, with lighter margins. Showy, golden-yellow

110

Primula cuneifolia
Prunella vulgaris

Pyrola asarifolia
Pyrola secunda

111

flowers borne profusely. Found usually growing in tight crevices on shale cliffs along the seashore; also common on bare slopes above the timber line. All over Southeastern Alaska and northward. (Illus. p. 107.)

PRÌMULA (*Primula veris,* the "first in spring" was an old appellation of one or more of the species). Primulaceae. "Primrose."

P. cuneifolia. An interesting little tufted dwarf, scarcely two inches tall; leaves cuneiform or wedge-shaped. One to three relatively large flowers on the 1–2-inch scape. Petals notched deeply; yellow eye. Found only at very high altitudes. Near Juneau only the magenta-flowered form has been found; the mountains near Seward produce the albino form only. Sometimes aptly called "Pixy Eyes." (Illus. p. 110.)

P. eximia. A tufted form which grows profusely in the tundra of the Arctic regions, particularly around Nome and along the Coast further north. The foliage produces a basal mound and from this arise a number of scapes with a cluster of characteristic Primula blossoms at the top, 3–6 inches. Slightly fragrant. Pale lavender.

PRUNELLA (spelling used by Linnaeus; also Brunella, pre-Linnaean, probably from old Greek *breune* or *braune,* "quinsy," which it is thought to cure). Labiatae.

P. vulgaris. "Self-Heal," "Heal-All." Common in Southeastern Alaska, where it grows along the roadsides and waste places, often quickly covering the scars left by the road builders. Flower heads purple, erect on 2–6-inch stems. A characteristic is the two opposite leaves just below the flower head. (Illus. p. 110.)

PULSATILLA Ludoviciana (also known as *Anemone patens*). "Wild Crocus." The large, lavender, globular blossoms, with their gold centers, resemble the garden crocus, to which plant it is in no way related. The plant appears very early in the spring, well protected by its fur-covered sepals and

112

involucre. As spring advances it follows the disappearance of the snow up the mountain slopes, blooming in clumps among the rocks or in open grassland. The flowers are followed by a long-plumed style. Eastern Interior.

PYROLA (a diminutive of Pyrus, the "pear tree," from some fancied resemblance in the foliage). Pyrolaceae. "Wintergreen," "Shinleaf."

Of the numerous species in Alaska all are low perennials, with running subterranean roots and a cluster of evergreen leaves, thick and leathery. Growing mostly in shaded and peaty soil.

P. asarifolia. One of the most showy of the Alaska species. Its racemes of nodding, pinkish flowers, touched with bright rose, are borne profusely. Valued as a cut flower, it remains attractive for a long time after being cut. Flower sprays are arching and graceful. This is sometimes called "Wild Lily-of-the-Valley." (Illus. p. 111.)

P. minor. Red stems and the entire flower a delicate rose pink. Somewhat like *P. asarifolia,* but the blossoms are smaller and less open, forming tight little bells. This species appears to endure more sun than any of the others. It is often found in the open along sandy roadsides, growing in loam rather than in leaf mold and moss as do the other species. Fibrous roots.

P. secunda. Interesting but not showy. Flowers greenish, which are strung along one side of the stem. (Illus. p. 111.)

All of the species named are common in Southeastern Alaska.

P. uniflora. See *Moneses uniflora.*

Other species of Pyrola found in Alaska are: *P. bracteata, P. chlorantha, P. elliptica,* and *P. uliginosa,* all found in Mount McKinley Park and elsewhere in the Interior. *P. aphylla* is a distinct species found at Buckland and Shungnak.

Rhinanthus Crista-gallii
Rhodiola integrifolia

Ribes bracteosum
Ribes lacustre

Ribes laxiflorum
Romanzoffia sitchensis

Rosa nutkana
Rubus Chamaemorus

117

Rubus parviflorus
Rubus pedatus

Rubus spectabilis
Rubus stellatus

119

RANUNCULUS (Latin name for "little frog"; applied to the genus by Pliny in allusion to the wet places in which many of the species grow). Ranunculaceae. "Buttercup," "Crowfoot." This genus is well represented among Alaska flowers. They are too well known to merit a lengthy description.

R. acris. A roadside weed; King Cove.

R. Bongardii. Weedy. Juneau.

R. Cymbalaria. Small, tufted plants; flowers on 3-inch stems; produces runners. Grows in wet soil. Southeastern Alaska and the Interior.

R. delphinifolia. Grows in shallow water and mud. A large plant of the Interior.

R. Eschscholtzii. Looks something like an Anemone, with cluster of leaves below the flower. Small, tufted alpine. Southeastern Alaska and the Interior.

R. hyperboreus. Slender, trailing; grows on the edges of ponds. Juneau to the Interior.

R. nivalis. A small alpine of the Interior.

R. occidentalis. The common meadow Buttercup of Southeastern Alaska. Upright plant with many branches. Characteristic lacquered yellow flowers.

R. pennsylvanicus. Large weedy plant of the Interior.

R. Purshii. Slender, trailing; grows around ponds. Interior.

R. pygmaeus. High alpine. Tiny tuft, never over 2 inches. Juneau and the Interior.

R. repens. Has long runners, rooting at joints. Southeastern Alaska.

R. reptans. Very small, slender; leaves grass-like. Muddy banks. Southeastern Alaska.

Other species found in Alaska are: *R. lapponicus, R. maconnii,* and *R. nelsonii.*

RHINANTHUS (Greek *rhis*, "a snout"; *anthos*, "a flower"). Scrophulariaceae. "Yellow Rattle," "Rattlebox."

R. Crista-gallii (R. groenlandicus). Branching stems to about 2 feet. Yellow flowers in upper leaf axils, much inflated in fruit. Leaves opposite, lance-shaped. Moist roadsides and casually about towns. Southeastern Alaska. (Illus. p. 114.)

RHODIOLA (Greek *rhodon*, "rose," because of rootstock exhaling a perfume of rose water). Also classed as *Sedum Rhodiola*. Crassulaceae.

R. integrifolia. "King's Crown," "Hen and Chickens." Cluster of stems 4–10 inches high, rising from one crown, erect and unbranched. Leaves glaucous and fleshy. Flowers dark brown or purplish in a terminal, flat-topped cyme. Found in practically every part of the Territory. (Illus. p. 114.)

RHODODENDRON (Greek *rhodon* and *dendron*, "rosetree"). Ericaceae. Very ornamental, broad-leaved, evergreen shrub.

R. camtschaticum. Larger than *R. lapponicum*. Leaves and flower-stems hairy. Flowers deep magenta, 1½ inches in diameter. Interior.

R. lapponicum. An alpine shrub of the Interior. Dwarf, dense-growing. Flowers 1 inch in diameter. Rose-purple clusters at the end of stems.

RIBES (probably derived from *ribas*, the Arabic name for *Rheum Ribes*; or by some supposed to be the Latinized form of *Riebs*, an old German word for "Currant"). Saxifragaceae. "Currant," "Gooseberry."

Unarmed or prickly shrubs, deciduous; palmately lobed foliage. Esteemed partly for their more or less edible fruits and partly for their handsome flowers, fruits, or foliage. Alaska is particularly rich in species of this important shrub.

Sambucus pubens
Sanguisorba sitchensis

Saxifraga aestivalis
Saxifraga Lyallii

123

R. bracteosum. "Skunk Bush" of Southeastern Alaska. A vigorous species, with large leaves and clusters of berries sometimes 12 inches long. Fruit is black, with white bloom; very pungent odor and taste. (Illus. p. 115.)

R. glandulosum. Called "Skunk Currant" in the Interior, where it abounds. A prostrate shrub with red, bristly berries, of fetid odor.

R. hudsonianum. An upright shrub of the Interior, with attractive foliage which colors beautifully in the autumn. Black berries covered with glandular hairs.

R. lacustre. "Wild Gooseberry" of the Coast. Leaves very similar to those of the cultivated Gooseberry; vigorous growth. Plant very prickly; berries are shiny black. (Illus. p. 115.)

R. laxiflorum. One of the commonest and most attractive shrubs of the Coast region. Very similar to *R. hudsonianum* except that the branches of *R. laxiflorum* are prostrate, having almost the effect of a vine. Growth very graceful. (Illus. p. 116.)

R. triste. "Red Currant" of the Interior. Very similar to the cultivated garden Currant, but slightly more acid. This is the most valuable of the group.

ROMANZOFFIA (named in honor of Count Nicholas Romanzoff). Hydrophyllaceae. Delicate, dwarf perennial herbs, with the aspect of Saxifrage.

R. sitchensis. Rootstock tuberiferous. Mound of scallop-leaved basal foliage, long-petioled. Flower scapes to 6 inches, weak. Flowers profusely in racemes, almost hiding the foliage. Corolla funnel-shaped, cream with yellow throat. Likes moisture and shade and seeks its home on the banks of running streams. Its nickname, "Mist Maidens," is applied because of its frequent appearance so close to a mountain stream that it is wet by the misty spray. All of Southeastern Alaska. (Illus. p. 116.)

124

R. unalaschensis. Rootstock not tuberiferous. Less showy than the preceding. Smaller. Unalaska and, rarely, Southeastern Alaska.

ROSA (ancient Latin name). "Rose." Ornamental shrubs, with handsome foliage and flowers. Fruits are called "hips." Four species are found at Haines, including the following:

R. acicularis. The wild rose of the Interior, where it abounds. A much more handsome plant than *R. nutkana.* Fragrant flowers, deep rose and lasting.

R. nutkana. Sometimes called the "Sitka Rose." Found in Southeastern Alaska, but not common. Flowers 2–2½ inches across, light pink. Fruit globular, without neck. (Illus. p. 117.)

RUBUS (Latin name connected with *ruber,* "red"). Rosaceae. A large genus, with which Alaska is well represented, including Raspberries, Thimbleberries, and Nagoon Berries.

R. arcticus. A pink-flowered form of *R. Chamaemorus.* Common in the Interior.

R. Chamaemorus. "Cloudberry" or "Baked Apple Berry." Creeping branches, herbaceous. An inhabitant of peat bogs. Flowers large, white. Edible fruit composed of a few soft drupelets. When ripe, resemble baked apples in color and flavor. All along the Coast and in the Interior. (Illus. p. 117.)

R. parviflorus. "Thimbleberry", of Southeastern Alaska. Has large-lobed but undivided leaves and thimble-shaped, tasteless, red fruit. Vigorous, perennial canes. (Illus. p. 118.)

R. pedatus. "Trailing Raspberry." A very slender trailing species, with white flowers and fruit of 2–6 large red drupelets. Southeastern Alaska. (Illus. p. 118.)

R. spectabilis. "Salmonberry." Abundant in Southeastern Alaska. Strong perennial canes and stoloniferous rootstalk, spiny. Flowers pale magenta; fruit edible and good, large, yellow or dark red. (Illus. p. 119.)

126

Saxifraga nootkana
Saxifraga oppositifolia

Saxifraga tricuspidata
Senecio triangularis

127

R. stellatus. "Nagoon or Lagoon Berry." A herbaceous species of swamp and tundra, producing a fragrant red berry of excellent flavor. Much prized for jelly. Related to this and commoner in the Interior is *R. acaulis.* (Illus. p. 119.)

R. strigosus. "Red Raspberry." The same species as the garden Raspberry. Splendid flavor. Open woods and brushlands of the Interior.

RUMEX (Latin name of unknown origin). "Dock," "Sorrel." Bold, weedy herbs with strong roots; closely allied to the Rhubarb and the Knotweeds. The following are some of the Alaska species: *R. acetosella; R. arcticus fenestratus; R. crispus; R.'mexicanus; R. obtusifolius; R. occidentalis.*

SALIX (ancient Latin name of Willow). Salicaceae. "Willow." Deciduous trees and shrubs of interesting habit; flowers in catkins.

A number of species of large-shrub or small-tree form are indigenous to Alaska, readily identified by their typical Willow characteristics.

S. reticulata. One of the most abundant of the dwarf trailing forms of high elevations. Dense growth; large fluffy catkins.

SAMBUCUS (old Latin name for the Elder; also spelled Sabucus). Caprifoliaceae. "Elder."

S. pubens. Large coarse shrubs, with pithy shoots. Heavy, pinnate, dark-green leaves. Clusters of fragrant, creamy-white flowers, followed by inedible, scarlet fruit, much esteemed by the birds. Coast region. (Illus. p. 122.)

SANGUISORBA (Latin, "blood" and "drink up," from reputed styptic properties in folk-medicine). Strong-growing perennial; leaves similar to those of the Rose. "Burnet."

S. Menziesii. Stems 1–1½ feet, branching, terminating in dense, oblong spikes of reddish-purple flowers. Found near Craig, growing in wet places.

128

S. microcephala. Another species with reddish-purple flowers. Grows in all parts of the Territory.

S. sitchensis. Fragrant white flowers. Grows in all parts of the Territory. (Illus. p. 122.)

SAUSSUREA (named after Theodor de Saussure or his father, Horace Benoit de Saussure, Swiss alpine travelers and scientists). Compositae.

S. americana. Tall; wide, spear-shaped, toothed leaves. Big terminal heads of rose-purple flowers. Southeastern Alaska.

S. densa. Well-named, as whole plant is dense-growing and dwarf. Interior.

S. monticola. Loose heads of flowers in flat umbels. Most showy of the species; moderately fragrant. Slender lance-shaped leaves. Interior.

SAXIFRAGA (Latin "rock" and "to break"; said by some to refer to the fact that many of the species grow in clefts of rock; by others to the supposition that certain species would cure stone in the bladder). Saxifragaceae. "Saxifrage," "Rockfoil." A genus of small plants, well represented in Alaska.

S. aestivalis. "Summer-flowering saxifrage." Grows 6–12 inches tall; rhizome rather stout and woody; leaves forming a basal rosette; round and neatly scalloped; channeled petioles. Flowers small, white, with red dots, in a terminal spike; seed pods dark red, persistent. Southeastern Alaska. (Illus. p. 123.)

S. bronchialis (S. austromontana). Very dwarf; stiff leaves, with a sharp point at the tip. Flowers pale yellow, with red dots, on 3-inch stems. All along Coast and in the Interior.

S. caespitosa. Low, tufted. Each stem springing from the crown has its individual whorl of stiff leaves at the base. Flowers pale yellow. Portions of Southeastern Alaska.

Silene acaulis
Silene noctiflora

Sisyrinchium littorale
Solidago multiradiata

S. flagellaris. A distinctive species of the Interior. From 1 to 8 inches high; densely glandular-hairy. The plant is stoloniferous, the stolons bearing a minute bud and roots at their apex. Flowers large, golden yellow. Wet alpine locations.

S. hieracifolia. Basal clump of large leaves; flower-stems often 18 inches. Sessile white flowers in a spike. Interior.

S. Hirculus. A striking species, with brilliant yellow, large blossoms. Tufted, with finely divided foliage. Grows in tundra in the northern sections.

S. Lyallii. Height 4–15 inches. Leaves cuneate or wedge-shaped, spreading from a short petiole. Small white flowers similar to those of a number of species, on smooth stems. (Illus. p. 123.)

S. Nelsonii. Very much the appearance of *S. aestivalis,* except that flowers grow in close head. Along the northern Coast.

S. nivalis. Very similar to *S. Lyallii.*

S. nootkana. A very attractive form, abundant in Southeastern Alaska. Has the characteristic panicle of small white flowers, freckled with red or brown, on a hairy stem. Flat, wheel-like tufts of spear-shaped, deeply toothed foliage. In rich soil the flower-stem grows stout and thickly branching, with numerous blossoms; but it is usually found along shale cliffs where there is little soil, and where it is fragile and dainty. (Illus. p. 126.)

S. oppositifolia. "Red Moss." A distinctive species, lacking the friendly adaptability of the other Alaska species, and very difficult to transplant. Grows usually on steep inaccessible cliffs. Dense-growing, trailing; dark-green, opposite leaves having the appearance of "French knots" in needlework. Flowers showy, bright magenta, borne singly on very short stems. Southwestern and Southeastern Alaska. (Illus. p. 126.)

S. punctata. Another species very similar to *S. aestivalis.* Aleutian Islands.

S. serpyllifolia. Tiny, tufted. Stems very seldom over 2 inches. Bright yellow. Northern Coast.

S. Tolmieii. Beautiful, distinct alpine species of Southeastern Alaska. Innumerable small white flowers on stems 1–3 inches tall. Leaves small and fleshy, thickly disposed on flat runners, spreading in large mats.

S. tricuspidata. Very similar to *S. bronchialis,* the only difference being in the shape of the leaf; the leaf of this species has three sharp points at the tip instead of one. Common in Southeastern Alaska. (Illus. p. 127.)

Other Saxifrages of the Territory are: *S. Mertensiana, S. reflexa,* and *S. unalaschensis.*

SCORZONELLA (old French, *scorzon,* "serpent"). Compositae.

S. borealis. Bright yellow daisy, 1–1½ inches in diameter. Long, slender stems a foot tall; slender, lanceolate leaves. Showy and good. Found in wet meadows. Southeastern Alaska.

SENECIO (Latin name, ultimately from *senex,* "old man," alluding to the hoary pappus). Compositae.

S. frigidus. Densely growing, downy, high alpine, with relatively large yellow ray flowers. Interior.

S. hyperborealis. An attractive, small-branching species. Numerous stems springing from the basal tuft. Flowers rich yellow.

S. lugens. Flowers small, in panicles. Has somewhat the appearance of a Goldenrod. About 2 feet high. Interior.

S. palustris. From 1 to 3 feet. Thick stem, clothed with deeply toothed leaves. Flowers in a terminal corymb.

S. pauciflorus. Grows in rather dry soil of the Interior. Basal cluster of foliage; small flowers in a corymb at the end of an almost bare stem, 2 feet or so high.

S. Pseudo-arnica. Bold plants growing in sand and gravel near the seashore. Stem very leafy, hairy. Few large flowers in a terminal cluster. All along the Coast.

Spiraea acuminata
Streptopus amplexifolius

Swertia perennis
Tellima grandiflora

135

Thalictrum alpinum
Tiarella trifoliata

S. resedifolius. A fragile little high alpine of the Interior. Flowers borne singly on 3–5-inch stems; deep orange.

S. triangularis. A tall weedy plant of wet alpine meadows, from Talkeetna south. Distinctive triangular leaf. Large terminal head of small yellow flowers. (Illus. p. 127.)

SIBBALDIA (named for Robert Sibbald, Scotch naturalist). Rosaceae.

S. procumbens. Low-growing. Flowers pale yellow, small and inconspicuous. Very attractive pale-green foliage; leaflets three, wedge-shaped, 3-toothed at the apex. Southeastern Alaska.

SILENE (Greek name of Bacchus' companions, described as covered with foam; also connected with *sialon,* "saliva," referring to the stickiness of the stem and calyx of some species). Caryophyllaceae.

S. acaulis. "Cushion Pink," "Moss Campion." Moss-like, tufted. Flowers almost stemless, varying from light pink to deep rose, rarely white. Long, strong roots which anchor the plant firmly on the high outcroppings of rock on mountain summits. Wide range in many parts of the Territory. (Illus. p. 130.)

S. Menziesii. Leafy, branching stems. Two opposite leaves at each branch of the stem. Small white flowers in terminal panicle. Southeastern Alaska.

S. noctiflora. A somewhat weedy plant, with lax leafy branches often 1–2 feet long. The blossoms are white, borne in the forks of the branches, opening only at night. Calyx much inflated; petals 2-cleft. Spreads widely over open waste spaces. (Illus. p. 130.)

S. repens. Leafy stems about 8 inches. Flowers with long calyx, in clusters at end of stem. Few root leaves. Southeastern Alaska.

138

Tofieldia coccinea
Trientalis arctica

Unifolium Eschscholtzianum
Vaccinium ovalifolium

SISYRINCHIUM (an old Greek name first applied to some other plant). Iridaceae. "Blue-Eyed Grass," "Rush Lily," "Grass Widow." Produces a thick clump of rush-like foliage. Flowers small, purplish-blue, from 5 to 15 inches high, several at end of a two-edged stem, protected by two sheathing, leaf-like bracts, the outer of which is about twice as long as the inner. The structure of the flower is much like that of the Iris except that the style branches are filiform instead of petal-like as in the Iris. The flowers open only when the sun is shining. Southeastern Alaska. (Illus. p. 131.)

SMILACINA (resembling Smilax). Liliaceae. Close to Streptopus and Unifolium.

S. sessilifolia. "False Solomon's Seal." Grows 12–18 inches tall. Stems slender and flexuous. Small white flowers in racemes. Fruit lined with black, becoming red. Interior.

SOLIDAGO (according to Gray, from *solidus*, "to make solid" or "draw together," in allusion to reputed healing properties). Compositae. "Goldenrod."

S. multiradiata. Varies greatly as to height. Near glaciers and at high altitudes very dwarf and tufted. Attains 2 feet or more in deep soil, where it is often found along roadsides. Typical Goldenrod flower in a terminal bunch. Southeastern Alaska and the Interior. (Illus. p. 131.)

Other Alaska species are: *S. elongata, S. lepida,* and *S. oreophila.*

SORBUS (ancient Latin name). Rosaceae. Deciduous trees or shrubs, with handsome foliage, attractive white flowers, and ornamental red fruit. "Mountain Ash," "Dogberry." Closely allied to Pyrus.

S. sitchensis. Small tree or shrub. Pinnate foliage with 7–17 leaflets. Small white flowers in loose corymbs, followed by showy, round red berries, which remain on the branches all winter if not eaten by birds. Common in Southeastern Alaska, rarely in the Interior.

SPIRAEA (ancient Greek name of a plant used for garlands, derived from *Speira*, band, wreath; probably used for the present genus by Clusius). Rosaceae. Subfamily, Spiraceae.

S. acuminata. Beautiful, 3–6 feet tall. Dies back each year and sprouts again from the crown. Large, compound, lanceolate leaves. Terminal flowers in panicles often a foot long, creamy-white. Southeastern Alaska. Rarely in the Interior. (Illus. p. 134.)

S. Menziesii. Upright shrub about 4 feet. Leafy branches. Leaves oblong, flowers pink, in long terminal racemes. Only in southern part of Territory.

S. Stevenii. Showy shrub of upright growth; leaves oval, pale olive green. Flowers white with pinkish tint in terminal corymbs. Interior, extending to parts of Southeastern Alaska.

SPIRANTHES (Greek referring to the twisted stalk). Orchidaceae. "Ladies' Tresses."

S. Romanzoffianum. Stem 6–15 inches high, leafy below; small flowers, white or greenish, in a twisted spike. Southeastern Alaska and the Interior.

STREPTOPUS (Greek, "twisted stalk," referring to the peduncles). Liliaceae. "Twisted Stalk."

S. amplexifolius. Stems arising 12 inches to 3 feet from a stout rootstock. Leaves clasping; flowers at axils, nodding, bell-shaped, creamy. Followed by a large, round, dark-red berry which is inedible. Stems branching. Southeastern Alaska. (Illus. p. 134.)

S. roseus. More dwarf than the preceding. Flowers dark red. Berry clear red, three-sided at first and becoming round when fully ripe. Stems solitary. Southeastern Alaska.

SWERTIA (named for Emanuel Swert, a bulb cultivator of Holland). Also spelled *Sweertia.* Gentianaceae.

S. perennis. Perennial, 1 to 2 feet. Opposite lance-shaped leaves. Gray-blue flowers in terminal racemes. Five-pointed petals, fringed at the base. Open bogs. Southeastern Alaska. (Illus. p. 135.)

Vaccinium uliginosum
Vaccinium Vitis-idea

Valeriana sitchensis
Veratrum Eschscholtzii

143

SYNTHYRIS (Greek, "together" and "little door" or "valve," referring to the valves of the seed capsule). Scrophulariaceae.

S. borealis. Tufted alpine plant about 8 inches high. Hairy leaves, mostly basal; stem leaves reduced and bract-like. Small flowers blue, in terminal racemes. Interior.

TELLIMA (anagram of Mitella). Saxifragaceae. Both Mitella and Tellima bear the vernacular name of "Bishop's Cap."

T. grandiflora. Round leaves, beautifully lobed and toothed. Whole plant glandular. Calyx inflated, bell-shaped, recurved. Inconspicuous greenish petals. Flowers scattered along tall stem. Large mound of basal foliage. Southeastern Alaska. (Illus. p. 135.)

THALICTRUM (perhaps from Greek *thallo*, "to grow green"). Ranunculaceae. "Meadow Rue." Erect perennial herbs with fern-like foliage and small flowers in panicles.

T. alpinum. Stems slender, smooth, naked, 3–5 inches high from a scaly rootstock. Leaves tufted at the base, twice 3–5 parted. Small flowers in a raceme; sepals greenish, yellow stamens. Southeastern Alaska. (Illus. p. 136.)

T. sparsiflorum. Stem 1–3 feet, branching. Glaucous leaves, something like Columbine. Small, greenish flowers in long panicles. Coast region.

THELYPTERIS. Polypodiaceae. A genus of small feathery ferns.

T. Dryopteris. Very slender, frail stalks, 8–12 inches, above creeping rootstock. Branches trifid; leaves pinnate or bi-pinnate, soft and thin. Grows in woods. Common from Ketchikan to Talkeetna. "Oak Fern."

T. Phegopteris. Stiffer than *T. Dryopteris* and simply bi-pinnate.

THUYA. Pinaceae. Evergreen trees.

T. plicata. "Red Cedar." Occurs only in Southeastern Alaska, and grows to considerable size. Used for lumber and shingles. Bark thin and fibrous, bright cinnamon in color. Branches flat; foliage in a flat spray, short, scale-like. Cones soon reflexed. Seed two on each scale.

TIARELLA (Latin, a "little tiara" or "turban," in reference to the form of the pistil). Saxifragaceae. "Foam Flower."

T. trifoliata. Compound leaves with three leaflets. Racemes of dainty white flowers; attractive; grows in shade. (Illus. p. 136.)

T. unifoliata. Similar except the leaves are united at the base.

Both are found in Southeastern Alaska.

TOFIELDIA (named after Tofield, a Yorkshire botanist). Liliaceae. "Lamb Lily." A plant with fibrous roots and leaves like a small German Iris.

T. coccinea. Growth tufted and very symmetrical, forming a round mound. Flowers on short stems above the foliage, small and inconspicuous, in a spike. Southeastern Alaska and the Interior. (Illus. p. 138.)

T. intermedia. Tall, iris-like. Grows in wet places. Flowers more showy than *T. coccinea,* white, with persistent seed pods, which are pink. Craig to Matanuska.

T. occidentalis. Similar to *T. intermedia.* Southeastern Alaska.

T. palustris. Same as *T. coccinea,* except that flower stalks are longer and it grows in wet soil. Interior.

TRIENTALIS (Latin for "the third of a foot"; referring to the height of the plant). Primulaceae. "Star Flower."

T. arctica. Grows 3–5 inches tall. Rhizome slender, creeping; stems solitary, slender, erect. Leaves whorled below the flower; flower white, star-shaped. Along the entire Coast. (Illus. p. 138.)

Veronica Wormskjoldii
Viburnum pauciflorum

Viola glabella
Viola Langsdorfii

147

TSUGA (Japanese name). Pinaceae. "Hemlock." Evergreen, cone-bearing trees.

T. heterophylla. "Western Hemlock." Composes nearly three-fourths of the forest cover in Southeastern Alaska. Short, somewhat pendulous branches. Head drooping in young trees.

T. Mertensiana. "Mountain Hemlock." Smaller-growing. Leaves spirally arranged around the branches. Grows mostly on the higher slopes. Southeastern Alaska.

UNIFOLIUM (Latin, "one leaf"). Liliaceae. "Wild Lily-of-the-Valley."

U. Eschscholtzianum. Spreading widely by means of underground stems running through soft mold, in shade. Leaves mostly 2 or 3, broad with long petiole, very like the true Lily-of-the-Valley. Small, white flowers in spikes, followed by mottled berries which later turn red. Southeastern Alaska. (Illus. p. 139.)

URTICA (classical name alluding to the "burning hairs"). Urticaceae. "Nettle." Herbs with stinging hairs. Greenish flowers in axillary cymes.

U. gracilis. Leaves lance-shaped, broad at the base, and pointed. Stems 1½–5 feet. Interior.

U. Lyalli. Leaves rounded, coarsely toothed. Common Coast form; also in the Interior.

VACCINIUM (Latin *vacca,* "a cow," perhaps because a pasture plant). "Blueberry."

V. caespitosum. "Lowbush Blueberry." Low-growing; deciduous; flowers appear before the leaves. Fruit blue, with bloom, of excellent flavor. Entire Coast region.

V. membranaceum. "Mountain Bilberry." Grows sparingly in Southeastern Alaska, along with *V. ovalifolium* and *V. parvifolium.* Usually 3–5 feet tall; deciduous. Fruit shiny black, round, and flattened; rather tasteless and non-acid.

V. ovalifolium. Tall Blueberry, deciduous. The tall, prolific Blueberry of Southeastern Alaska, 2–8 feet; bark red; flowers pink bells before the leaves appear. Fruit blue with bloom. Excellent. (Illus. p. 139.)

V. parvifolium. "Red Huckleberry." Leaves sometimes evergreen. Flowers white bells, appearing after the leaves. Fruit transparent red, pleasantly acid. Southeastern Alaska.

V. uliginosum. The common Blueberry of the Interior, where it is very variable as to height. Deciduous; flowers appear before the leaves. Fruit blue, with bloom, of excellent quality. In Southeastern Alaska grows mostly at high altitudes, where it is much dwarfed. (Illus. p. 142.)

V. Vitis-idea. "Lowbush Cranberry." A bog species; dwarf, matted growth; thick, oval evergreen leaves. Flowers in terminal clusters, pink. Fruit red. Good. Along Coast and in parts of the Interior. (Illus. p. 142.)

VALERIANA (Latin *valeo,* "to be strong," in allusion to medicinal uses). Valerianaceae. "Wild Heliotrope." Perennial herbs, with strong-scented roots. Leaves opposite.

V. capitata. Similar to *V. sitchensis,* except much less robust, and flowers in compact heads. Entire Coast region and parts of the Interior, growing in wet subalpine locations.

V. septentrionalis. Slender-growing; small leaves; flowers in loose panicles. Meadows around Fairbanks.

V. sitchensis. Compound leaves of 3–5 segments, the terminal segment much the largest. White flowers, pinkish in bud. Alpine meadows of Southeastern Alaska and the Interior. Flowers and roots fragrant. (Illus. p. 143.)

VERATRUM (ancient name of Hellebore). "False Hellebore." Liliaceae.

V. Eschscholtzii. Rhizome stout; stem erect, stout; leafy base thickened but not truly bulbous. A bold plant often attaining 10 feet. Leaves broad, veined, and pleated, contracted to a broad sheath. Greenish flowers in long terminal panicle. Wet alpine pastures of Southeastern Alaska. (Illus. p. 143.)

Viola palustris
Woodsia glabella

VERONICA (named in honor of St. Veronica). Scrophulariaceae. "Speedwell." Hardy herbs with opposite leaves.

V. americana. Strong-growing and spreading from trailing stems, which root where they touch the ground. Axillary flowers blue. Ditches and wet places, Southeastern Alaska.

V. serpyllifolia. Slender, erect, growing in clumps, the base prostrate and rooting. Flowers very pale blue, with deeper stripes. Southeastern Alaska.

V. Wormskjoldii. Somewhat similar to *V. serpyllifolia,* but stronger-growing. Flowers dark blue, campanulate. Interior, and Southeastern Alaska at high altitudes. (Illus. p. 146.)

VIBURNUM (ancient Latin name). Caprifoliaceae. Deciduous shrubs.

V. pauciflorum. Tall, deciduous shrub of straggling growth, with opposite, corrugated leaves; flowers small, in terminal, few-flowered cymes. Fruit scarlet, edible. Grows in shade and in moist, porous soil. Southeastern Alaska. "Highbush Cranberry." (Illus. p. 146.)

VIOLA (classical name). Violaceae. Easily identified. Besides the conspicuous blossoms which appear in the spring, there are aften produced later, inconspicuous, bud-like cleistogamous flowers, which are often more fruitful than the ordinary blossoms.

V. adunca. Rootstock woody, erect. Flowers blue, often with pale base. Southwestern Alaska.

V. biflora. Small yellow violet at Nome and along northern coast. Leaves round. Stem often bearing two flowers, citrous yellow, with distinct penciling.

V. glabella. The lovable little yellow violet of the Coast. Sometimes called "Johnny-Jump-Up." One of the first flowers to appear in the spring. Stems erect but weak. Flowers springing from axils of leaves. Grows in shady woods. (Illus. p. 147.)

V. Langsdorfii. A distinctive and important Southeastern Alaska species. Flowers deep blue. Tufted growth. Stems sometimes 8 or 10 inches long when growing in tall grass. (Illus. p. 147.)

V. palustris. As the name implies, a water-loving species, growing in wet meadows and light shade. Slender, jointed rootstock, stoloniferous. Leaves round; flowers pale lavender. Widely distributed along the Coast and also in the Interior. (Illus. p. 150.)

WAHLBERGELLA. Caryophyllaceae.

W. apetala. Slender-growing; stems 6–10 inches, with few lance-shaped leaves. Inflated calyx; purplish flower at end of stem. Interior.

W. Drummondii (also known as *Lychnis Drummondii*). Many tall, slender stems springing from one crown. Flower-stems branching. Inflated calyx, with 10 dark stripes. Interior.

WOODSIA (after John Woods, an English botanist). Polypodiaceae. A genus of rock-loving ferns.

W. glabella. Low, tufted, pinnate fronds. Thin, delicate; growing on moist rocks. Southeastern Alaska. (Illus. p. 150.)

YOUNGIA. Compositae.

Y. nana. Densely tufted alpine, with one long taproot. Tuft of leaves thickly covered with small white daisies. Interior.

ZYGADENUS (Greek "yoke" and "gland," some of the species having two glands in the base of the perianth). Liliaceae. "Wand Lily."

Z. chloranthus is reported from Mount McKinley Park, but this is probably synonymous with *Z. elegans*.

Z. elegans (also *Anticlea elegans*). Sometimes 3 feet tall. Abundant, grass-like foliage, broad and very glaucous, usually basal. Flowers greenish, opening about ½ inch across, in loose racemes at top of stout stem. Common in the Interior and the northern Coast region.

INDEX

[NOTE: This index includes synonyms, vernacular names, and miscellaneous references not in alphabetical order in text. Alphabetized scientific names and illustrations are not included.]

153